A Gu
to the
Lectionary
for
Masses *with* Children

With Suggestions for Weekday Masses
During the School Year

Peter Mazar
Robert Piercy

LTP

Liturgy Training Publications

Liturgy Training Publications
1800 North Hermitage Avenue
Chicago IL 60622-1101

Order Phone: 1-800-933-1800
FAX: 1-800-933-7094
Editorial Offices: 1-312-486-8970

This book was designed and typeset by Phyllis Martinez of Martinez Partners. The book cover was designed by Judy Sweetwood. The illustrations throughout this book were selected from *Clip Art* by St. Louis artist Steve Erspamer, SM. This collection of over 1500 reproducible illustrations has been gathered by the artist into separate volumes for Years A, B and C. *Clip Art* is available from LTP.

Printed in the United States of America.
ISBN 1-56854-043-4
G/LMC
$8.95

Contents

Before *you* Read *this* Book

Soon after the September 1, 1993, publication of the *Lectionary for Masses with Children,* many folks called LTP with questions — good ones — about using this new ritual book of the church.

In this guide we try to answer a number of these questions. The answers form the first part of this book. Then, later in the book, we make suggestions for weekday Masses through the school year.

Our answers and suggestions rely heavily on the Introduction to the children's lectionary, which was prepared by the Committee on the Liturgy of the National Conference of Catholic Bishops. There is no shortcut to reading it. It has been reprinted in this guide, and begins on page 104.

Another document filled with answers to questions is the *Directory for Masses with Children.* This was published in 1973 by the Roman Congregation for Divine Worship. It is fundamental reading for those who prepare liturgy — with children, with adults, with anyone. It too has been reprinted here, and begins on page 92.

Liturgy has its spirit, and that can be hard to get across in writing. This is one reason liturgical documents, such as the Introduction to the children's lectionary, are written primarily to communicate principles rather than rules. And that is why it can be hard to search through a document to find a particular rule or guideline.

The book you have in your hands was put together to focus on guidelines, but, truth to tell, the principles and spirit of the liturgy are a lot more important than specific

rules. When someone has caught this spirit, the rules fall into perspective. This spirit makes so many words unnecessary.

We begin this guide with something of an apology. We found it tedious to repeat the titles *Lectionary for Mass* (which is the book containing the readings used at Mass on Sundays and other occasions) and *Lectionary for Masses with Children.* So we often substituted the phrases "regular lectionary" and "children's lectionary." But these phrases have problems.

On the one hand, the *Lectionary for Mass* — the "regular lectionary" — isn't just for adults. It's for everyone. The *Lectionary for Masses with Children* is like a supplement; if the circumstances are right, the readings in the children's lectionary are used in place of the readings in the regular lectionary.

On the other hand, the *Lectionary for Masses with Children* — the "children's lectionary" — isn't only for Masses where the majority of the people are children. Paragraph 12 of the Introduction tells us that this lectionary "may be used at Sunday Masses when a large number of children are present along with adults, or when the children have a separate liturgy of the word, or for Masses at which most of the congregation consists of children (for example, school Masses)."

Keep in mind that it's always permissible to use the "regular" *Lectionary for Mass,* even if everyone in the congregation is a child. In fact, at times it may be best to use the regular lectionary if the children are old enough to comprehend it.

Remember that the *Lectionary for Masses with Children* is used within that special kind of liturgy called "Mass with children," which is a Mass adapted to the needs of preadolescents. This kind of liturgy has its own spirit, its own guidelines, even its own eucharistic prayers. These guidelines are given in the *Directory for Masses with Children.*

Two resources to help the parish and school staff make good use of the *Directory* are LTP's *The Welcome Table,* by Elizabeth Jeep, and GIA/LTP's *Leader's Manual* of the *Hymnal for Catholic Students,* by Gabe Huck and several

other contributors. (Part of the *Leader's Manual* is about the hymnal, but most of it is about the practical ins and outs of preparing liturgy.)

For other resources from LTP, check the bibliography on page 127 in this guide book.

The term "Masses *with* children" is deliberate. "*For* children" might make it sound as if all ages are not welcome to participate at such a Mass.

Of course, "with children" can sound a bit odd, too. Every Mass can be "with children." Every liturgy, in mystery, is a gathering of the whole church, of people of every age — even those who have died! All the baptized are welcome. All of us have a place at the supper of the Lamb.

Questions & Answers

We aren't sure about buying the *Lectionary for Masses with Children.* Is it official?

Over the years, several books called "children's lectionaries" were published in the United States. A couple of these had the temporary approval of the Bishop's Committee on the Liturgy (something that was always stated in the book itself). Others were unauthorized.

Now the Roman Catholic Church in the United States has an official children's lectionary, approved by the bishops and confirmed by Rome. This lectionary is based on an approved translation of the Bible, and an excellent one at that.

With the publication of this official *Lectionary for Masses with Children,* the bishops have withdrawn the temporary approval given to any other children's lectionary.

What Bible translation does this lectionary come from?

It is called the *Contemporary English Version* of the Bible. The American Bible Society prepared this translation. The *Contemporary English Version* is not a paraphrase of the Bible but a fresh translation from the original languages.

By the end of 1993 the American Bible Society had published only the New Testament with the Books of Psalms and Proverbs. The rest of the Bible has been scheduled for publication soon.

What age group is the children's lectionary for?

Paragraph 15 of the Introduction to the *Lectionary for Masses with Children* says, "The hearers of the word for whom this [lectionary] is primarily intended are children of elementary grades (preadolescents)."

Most eighth-graders are capable of comprehending the readings in the regular lectionary, so there probably is no need to use the children's lectionary if Mass is celebrated with mostly eighth-graders. Most third-graders probably are not capable of comprehending the readings in the regular lectionary, and so the children's lectionary would be useful in preparing Mass for an assembly of mostly third-graders.

Of course, Mass with mixed ages can strike a balance. Something especially fine about the *Lectionary for Masses with Children* is that its language is simple but not juvenile. That's important, because even small children do not like being talked down to. You can use this lectionary with people of all ages without excluding anyone.

Why are there different volumes of the children's lectionary?

LTP has published the children's lectionary in four volumes — a single volume for weekdays and three volumes for Sundays, one for Year A, one for Year B, one for Year C. Dividing the lectionary into four volumes makes each volume easier to carry and use.

There also are "study editions" of each volume. These are smaller and less expensive editions that are not meant to be used at Mass. Instead, they are meant for study and rehearsal.

Year A? Year B? How do I know what year we're in?

The lectionary for Sunday Mass is divided into three years: A, B and C. On most Sundays in "A" years (1996, 1999, 2002, etc.), the church reads from Matthew's gospel. On most Sundays in "B" years (1994, 1997, 2000, etc.) we read through Mark, and in "C" years (1995, 1998, 2001, etc.) we read through Luke. (John's gospel is read every year especially during Lent and Eastertime.)

Just bear in mind that lectionary years begin on the First Sunday of Advent (the fourth Sunday before

Christmas), not on January 1. So November 27, the First Sunday of Advent in 1994, is the beginning of Year C, which lasts through 1995 and ends on November 26, the solemnity of Christ thc King (which is the Sunday before Advent).

The lectionary has page numbers but it also has other numbers. What are these?

These are "lectionary numbers." They are shorthand to help someone refer to sets of readings. For instance, in the children's lectionary the number for the readings for the First Sunday of Lent in Year A is 18. In Year B it's 19. In Year C it's 20.

(In the regular lectionary, the number for the First Sunday of Lent in Year A is 22. So the numbers in the children's lectionary do not match the numbers in the regular lectionary.)

You will not, of course, find every lectionary number in each volume of the children's lectionary. For instance, the volume for Sundays in Year A has numbers 1, 4, 7, and so on. Year B has 2, 5, 8, and so on. Year C has 3, 6, 9, and so on. (In all the volumes the lectionary numbers increase from front to back, as you would expect.)

I'm searching for a particular Bible passage in the children's lectionary. How do I find it?

In the back of this guide, beginning on page 115, we have an index to the scripture readings in the children's lectionary. This index uses lectionary numbers, not page numbers, to refer to the readings.

For example, the index tells us that the gospel about the finding of the child Jesus in the Temple, Luke 2:41 – 51, can be found in three places, all of them in the weekday volume: #272 (for St. Joseph's Day), #303 (for the memorial of the Immaculate Heart) and #451 (in the Common of the Blessed Virgin Mary).

Are there times when I am obligated to use the children's lectionary and not the regular one?

In one word, no. In fact, ordinarily you would use the regular lectionary if the readings seem suited to the comprehension of the people gathered for Mass.

Whether or not to use the children's lectionary is a necessary judgment call. On the one hand, children are being introduced to the scriptures, and the regular *Lectionary for Mass* was prepared to open up the richness of the Bible. On the other hand, the liturgy requires participation, and comprehension helps that happen.

The *Lectionary for Masses with Children* was prepared to help children better comprehend the scripture readings. It also was prepared, in its own words, because "the church intends to lead children into one community of faith, formed by the proclamation of the word of God" (12). In other words, the *Lectionary for Masses with Children* is meant to enable children to become active participants in parish worship.

Can adults read at Mass from the children's lectionary?

Yes. The key is ability, not age. Good reading is part natural talent and part acquired skill. Any reader is expected to proclaim God's word with competence and with dignity.

Paragraph 23 in the Introduction to the children's lectionary addresses this question:

> *It should not be presumed that children should proclaim the word of God in the celebrations in which this lectionary is used. Some younger children are able to read the scriptures competently, but the witness of older children, teenagers, or adults, ministering graciously and reverently to young children engaged in liturgical prayer, is more conducive to the children's growing reverence for the word of God than the peer ministry of embarrassed or ill-prepared children.*

Can readers read from a Bible at Mass instead of reading from a lectionary?

The *Directory for Masses with Children* (43) says that if all the readings assigned to the day seem unsuited to the capacity of the children, it is permissible to choose readings either from the *Lectionary of the Roman Missal* or directly from the Bible, but taking into account the liturgical seasons.

One problem with this permission is that reading out loud from a Bible can be clumsy — it can be easy to lose your place, and it might be difficult for your hearers to tell what is going on unless you identify pronouns or add a few details to the passage. For instance, you might need to inform everyone that Moses is standing on Mount Sinai when all of this happens, or that Jesus is speaking the words you are about to say. Lectionaries include these adjustments.

The *Lectionary for Masses with Children,* of course, is filled with readings suited "to the capacity of the children." The index (beginning on page 115) is a way to locate readings and to become more and more familiar with the riches of these volumes.

What if my choices of readings are a mistake? Is there a sure-fire way not to make a mistake?

This guidebook was prepared to help you. We cover some of the basics about the church seasons and church holidays. Know what day it is and what season it is. This is essential information to help direct your choices.

Something else to consider is the communal life of the children. What is going on in their lives? Are they preoccupied by some anxiety or event? Say, for instance, that it's Advent and that a member of the community has died recently. There are, of course, readings and psalms and hymns that touch upon both events.

In every season and on every feast, our fears and troubles and hopes and joys are brought before God. Perhaps the only serious "mistake" we can make is in failing to recognize the wholesomeness and depth of the scriptural and liturgical life that is ours in the church.

Psalms

I know that psalms are wonderful to sing and that we really should be singing them at Mass. Any advice?

If at all possible, sing the psalms the parish sings at Sunday Mass. That's probably better than teaching children their own melodies.

The psalms in the children's lectionary are from the *Contemporary English Version* of the Bible. Once composers publish music for this translation, perhaps some of this music can become part of the parish's repertory, instead of being melodies that children are taught and then later abandon as they grow up. However, many of the psalm refrains in the children's lectionary are the same as the refrains many parishes already sing on Sundays.

Psalms fall loosely into categories. There are songs of repentance, of sorrow, of marching to Jerusalem, of exile, of thanksgiving, of exultant praise, and of several other moods and images. Some are associated with Lent or with Eastertime or with another season or festival of the year.

Say that the psalm given in the lectionary is a psalm of praise, but you don't have a musical setting for it. You might substitute another psalm of praise from the ones the parish sings.

Psalm 122, "We shall go up with joy to the house of our God," fits the spirit of the liturgy from All Saints' Day right through to Advent. The lectionary offers it as a "common psalm for the last weeks of the year," which means that it may be used on Sundays and weekdays in place of other psalms. These "common psalms" for the seasons can be found in the back of the Sunday volumes of the children's lectionary.

Perhaps you do not have a good setting of Psalm 122. You might substitute one that has a similar spirit — for example, Psalm 126, "When from our exile God leads us home again, we'll think we're dreaming," or Psalm 84, "How lovely is your dwelling place."

Maybe the best way to get people to sing is to keep coming back to the same melodies — at every Mass during a stretch of weeks or during an entire season, and also from year to year. The repetition builds repertory.

I'm a parish priest who is not very adept at giving homilies to children. Are there alternatives?

The Introduction to the *Lectionary for Masses with Children* (10) has this to say:

> *Because the explanation of the scripture readings is so important at Masses with children, a homily should always be given. However, in order that they might not be deprived of the riches of God's word, especially if the priest finds it difficult to adapt himself to the mentality of children, and with the consent of the pastor or rector of the church, one of the adults participating in these celebrations may speak to the children after the gospel.*

SUNDAYS

Shouldn't Sunday Mass have three readings? In the children's lectionary I notice sometimes there are three readings for a Sunday but most times there only are two.

You are right in saying that the regular lectionary has three readings provided for Sunday Mass: there is the gospel and two readings before the gospel.

The *General Instruction of the Roman Missal* (318) gave the bishops the choice to require either one or two readings before the gospel at Mass on Sundays and solemnities. In the United States, the bishops decided that there should be two readings before the gospel.

But in the case of Masses with children, the *Directory for Masses with Children* (42) has this to add:

> *If three or even two readings appointed on Sundays or weekdays can be understood by children only with difficulty, it is permissible to read two or only one of them, but the reading of the gospel should never be omitted.*

The Introduction to the *Lectionary for Masses with Children*, 16 – 17, repeats these words (because they are important), and then goes on to say:

> *In the preparation of this lectionary, readings from the* Lectionary for Mass *which were judged to be too abstract were eliminated or shortened.*

That explains why the children's lectionary has only two readings for many Sundays. That is the church's decision, approved by the bishops and confirmed by the Roman Congregation for Divine Worship. So when circumstances allow the use of the children's lectionary, if it gives two readings for a Sunday, you would use those two.

On Sundays and holy days of obligation we have a separate liturgy of the word for young children. The children's lectionary seems perfect for us. Am I right?

You certainly are. Please review paragraphs 7 and 8 of the Introduction to the *Lectionary for Masses with Children.*

On Sundays the children's lectionary corresponds as much as possible with the readings in the regular lectionary. That means that even if adults and children have separate liturgies of the word, they will be hearing much the same scriptures. Keep in mind that a separate liturgy of the word with children *is* the liturgy of the word of the Mass. It is not a catechetical session.

Interestingly, paragraph 14 of the Introduction includes words of encouragement to households "to prepare together those readings which will be used in common both by the adults and the children . . . and to reflect after the celebration on the word proclaimed there." In some parishes, parents are being urged to purchase a copy of the children's lectionary. At home they can use the week's readings for prayer with their children.

Many people have misgivings about separating adults and children at Mass. Paragraph 11 of the Introduction counsels that the purpose of the children's lectionary is not to create a different liturgy for children but to "lead them to active, conscious, and authentic participation in the worship of the whole assembly."

We have a family Mass every Sunday. Can we use the children's lectionary at this Mass?

Some parishes, on occasion or every weekend, have a Sunday Mass geared to children and their families, who stay together to hear the same readings. The Introduction to the children's lectionary (13) has a rather challenging (and some would say troubling) paragraph that limits its use at these Masses:

> *Proper balance and consideration for the entire assembly should be observed. Therefore, priest celebrants should not use this* Lectionary for Masses with Children *exclusively or even preferentially at Sunday Masses, even though large numbers of children are present.*

The word "balance" is important here. At Sunday Masses in which adults and children stay together, it is not forbidden to use the Sunday readings from the children's lectionary, but this would happen only after weighing the needs of the entire congregation.

Note however that the same paragraph of the Introduction goes on to state that unless the children's lectionary is used at a separate liturgy of the word for children, it should never be used on Christmas, Epiphany, the Sundays of Lent, Easter Sunday, Ascension or Pentecost. These days are considered too important to modify the liturgy of the word for the entire congregation.

There is something else to consider in preparing a "family Mass." On the one hand it's good for a parish to do everything in its power to help build up families and family life. On the other hand, it can't be right to make one group of people welcome at Mass if that means making other groups less welcome. The ideal is to include everyone of every age and ability at Sunday worship.

In that inclusive spirit, the *Lectionary for Masses with Children* is not childish. The translation of the Bible used in this lectionary is comprehensible to children without being condescending to children or adults.

Some of my students do not go to Mass on Sundays. Would it be a good idea to use the Sunday readings at the weekday school Mass?

You can be confident that the weekday readings in the children's lectionary are rich fare; repeating the Sunday readings at weekday Mass only deprives everyone of the weekday readings.

If you are concerned that students have the benefit of breaking open the Sunday word, why not share the Lord's Day readings during the week in religion class? This might happen before Sundays, as preparation, or after Sundays, as reflection.

Perhaps your main concern is that the children do not attend Sunday Mass. Fostering attendance is a parish problem that a school tends to inherit. The school can help out by building enthusiasm not just for attendance — and lively participation — at Mass, but also for keeping Sundays holy. Here, as in other endeavors, households and the school can cooperate creatively to aim toward a goal.

Mass attendance is a good habit; either it's a part of our lives or it's not. The parish school is involved in helping children build all sorts of good habits and disciplines; religious observances are a part of these. Be creative. Some schools and religious education programs organize carpools to help students get to Mass.

Good school liturgies on weekdays can help students participate at parish liturgies on Sundays, especially if the school and parish staff work together to build up a common repertory of music and if the parish encourages students to join in the liturgical ministries as their abilities allow.

Weekdays

I understand how to use the Sunday lectionary, but this weekday one — there are so many options!

You're right. To use the weekday lectionary well you often will need to make careful choices from among several options.

You will need to choose the days to celebrate Mass with children. And you will need to choose which readings will be proclaimed those days.

An important aspect of liturgy preparation is knowing the options available to us. There are choices to be made from the lectionary, from the sacramentary (the book of the presider's words), from the psalms, from hymnals.

Of course, making choices means work. First, a person has to be familiar with the principles and regulations and especially the spirit of the liturgy. Then the options must be read and considered.

This is good work, challenging work, and those who prepare the liturgy really should become familiar with the options that the church provides. But all of this work takes time!

I'm a teacher. Once a month I am in charge of planning Mass. Where do I start?

You might start with the suggestions in this guidebook: Look over the page dealing with the season of the year, and then look over the suggestions for the two-week (or so) period in which you are going to be celebrating Mass. That's a beginning.

Of course, it usually isn't the Mass that needs the preparation as much as the participants. For the time of year, what sort of traditions are there from the past? What days were celebrated? What songs were sung? What scriptures were proclaimed?

If you often have the responsibility to prepare Mass, read through the *Directory for Masses with Children.* This was written for you. Also read through the Introduction to the *Lectionary for Masses with Children.* Both of these have been reprinted in this guide.

Another resource for parish and school personnel is GIA/LTP's *Leader's Manual* of the *Hymnal for Catholic Students.* We refer to it often in these pages. Even before you read it, you might just skim through its headlines — for example: "Liturgy is not about how we feel; it is about who we are and whose we are," "Liturgies are filled with processions," "The liturgy has times of silence," "Comments should be few, brief, prepared." The book is filled with basic considerations to mull over and to bring to bear on your preparations for liturgy.

The children's lectionary for weekdays has, and I'm quoting from the table of contents: "Weekday Readings," "Gospel Acclamations for Ordinary Time," "Proper of Saints," "Commons," "Sacraments," "Masses for Various Needs and Occasions." I'm having some trouble figuring out why all these things are in the same book.

Let's go over these parts one by one:

"Weekday Readings" are sets of readings offered for each season. You can use these on any weekday of that season unless it is a solemnity or feast; then you would use the readings for the day in the Proper of Saints. For instance, there are four sets of readings for weekdays in Advent. You can use these readings on any Advent weekday except the solemnity of the Immaculate Conception and the feast of Our Lady of Guadalupe.

In the sections for Advent, Lent and Eastertime, the gospel acclamations are found where you might expect — right before the gospels for each set of readings. However, during Ordinary Time you pick an acclamation from a "generic" list of them that follows the readings for Ordinary Time.

The "Proper of Saints" is where you'll find readings or suggestions for readings for the celebrations that come on the same day each year, such as All Saints' Day.

The "Commons" is like an appendix to the Proper of Saints. The Proper directs you to certain readings in the Commons. (The word "proper" here means "specific," and "common" means "generic.")

For example, on most of the martyrs' days the Proper of Saints tells you that you can choose readings from the "Common of Martyrs," where there are three options for a first reading; you would pick the one that you feel is most appropriate to the saint you are remembering that day. There is only one gospel passage in the Common of Martyrs. This gospel can be read on any martyr's day.

The section of the children's lectionary for weekdays titled "Sacraments," obviously enough, has readings for celebrations of the sacraments. Here, for instance, you'll find readings appropriate for first communion or for a communal penance service.

"Masses for Various Needs and Occasions" is a treasury of readings that can be used when needed, especially during Ordinary Time on any weekday that isn't a solemnity or feast. There are readings for special celebrations, such as the end of the school year, or for days when someone is sick or someone has died, or for a Mass in a time of war or other troubles.

I'm looking at the calendar days in the Proper of Saints. Some are ranked "solemnities," some "feasts," some "memorials," and some don't seem to have any rank. Explain this to me.

The rank indicates something of the importance of a day in the life of the church. If two days happen to coincide, one day usually outranks another. Sundays, for instance, always outrank memorials. (How a day's rank affects your choice of readings is the subject of the next question and answer. It's also the subject of the handy guidelines for selecting readings, which are found on pages 29 and 30.)

In the Proper of Saints, a saint's day without a rank means that the observance is optional; the parish can choose whether or not to keep that day. Sometimes there are two or more options for the same day. For instance, on October 16 the calendar says St. Hedwig and St. Margaret Mary Alacoque. So a parish and its school is free to celebrate Hedwig or Margaret Mary or neither of them.

But keep in mind that the church seasons, too, enter into the picture. For example, during Lent all memorials are optional, as the saints' days take a "back seat" to the holy season. Every special day of the church takes on the spirit of the season in which it is celebrated.

You don't have to guess whether or not a day is optional, or which day outranks what other day. Get yourself a good church calendar for the year, such as LTP's *Liturgy and Appointment Calendar.* A church calendar is essential for scheduling the year's liturgies.

How does a day's rank affect the choice of readings in the *Lectionary for Masses with Children*?

(Because this just might be the hardest question to answer, the guidelines for selecting readings for Mass have been summarized on pages 29 and 30.)

In general, the more important the day, the more important it is to read particular readings. That way the entire church is hearing the same scriptures on its most momentous days. On Sundays and solemnities, the children's lectionary includes specific readings for Mass. Those are the readings you must use if you use the children's lectionary.

On days ranked as feasts you also would use the day's readings. However, on many feasts the children's lectionary offers choices from the "Commons." For example, October 18 is the feast of St. Luke. The Proper of Saints gives a gospel (#396) that would be used at Mass that day, but then it tells you that the first reading is chosen from the Common of Apostles.

On days ranked as memorials and on the optional days that you observe, you have even more options. Either you can use readings to fit the memorial (as directed by the

Proper of Saints) or you can choose readings from the appropriate seasonal section. For instance, if it's Ordinary Time you can choose from the weekday options in the Ordinary Time section.

So, as an example, on October 17, the memorial of the martyred bishop Ignatius, the Proper of Saints says, "From the Common of Martyrs or the Common of Pastors." That means that you can choose readings from these sections for Mass this day. But you also can choose from the weekday readings for Ordinary Time.

On memorials within the church seasons of Advent, Christmastime, Lent and Eastertime, it's usually best to choose readings from the seasonal section rather than to choose from the options offered in the Proper of Saints.

For instance, you may be preparing a Mass for St. Nicholas's Day, December 6, a day that always falls during Advent. Instead of choosing from the Common of Pastors, as the Proper of Saints suggests, it might be more appropriate to choose from the options for Advent. The Advent readings fit the spirit of the season and of the saints of the season, too.

In the Proper of Saints there are brief instructions about which readings to choose to celebrate a saint's day. On some days the instructions get more specific than on other days. Why is that?

Sometimes a particular scripture reading fits a saint so well that it would be a loss not to hear it proclaimed on the saint's memorial.

For example, on January 26, the memorial of Timothy and Titus, it seems right to hear from one of the letters of Paul to either Timothy or Titus, and so two selections from these letters are given in the Proper of Saints, #248, as a possible first reading for the memorial. The gospel that day can be chosen from the Common of Pastors (as the Proper of Saints directs) or from any gospel reading for Ordinary Time.

Sometimes one of the readings in the Common sections is particularly appropriate to a saint. The lectionary may suggest its use on that day.

For instance, because Elizabeth of Hungary gave what she owned to the poor, on November 17 the lectionary suggests using the gospel in the Common of Saints that's designated "for those who work for the underprivileged" (#473-2, Matthew 25:31 – 40, "Whenever you did it for others, you did it for me").

What readings are used if the weekday is not a solemnity, feast or saint's day?

In Advent, Lent and Eastertime, use one of the sets of seasonal weekday readings. In Ordinary Time, use one of the sets of readings for Ordinary Time or, if there's a special need, use readings from the "Masses for Various Needs and Occasions."

As an example, in a time of war or of violence, on a weekday in Ordinary Time you might find it appropriate to use readings #513 – 517, "for peace and justice" (although set #224 in the weekday section for Ordinary Time also has appropriate readings).

However, to continue our example, if a time of war coincides with Advent, Christmastime, Lent or the Easter season, it may be best to choose appropriate readings from among the options offered for the season. That way the season itself helps to form our conscience and our prayer. In every season there are readings that speak to our hopes for an end to violence.

Why are there so many optional days, and why would we keep one and not another?

Many of the optional saints' days are religious founders, and so a saint's day may be dear to a religious community and to the parishes it serves. Some optional days are of saints beloved by certain nationalities, such as Januarius of Naples and Wenceslaus of Bohemia. Some are the saints of our hemisphere, such as Rose of Lima and Martin de Porres. And there are American saints, such as Rose Philippine Duchesne, whose memory is precious to many people in the Midwest.

LTP publishes a *Companion to the Calendar,* by Mary Ellen Hynes, a wonderful book for educators and families with information about every special day of the church year. Besides being a classroom resource, the information in the book can help the staff choose the occasions to celebrate with children.

Students have Mass once a week. A few times a year the entire school celebrates Mass together, but during most weeks the different grades go to Mass on different days. That's a lot of work to get ready. Can we use just one set of readings each week for all the grade levels?

You could do that, but there are a few things to consider. First, on a feast or solemnity, you really should be celebrating with the readings for the day.

A second consideration: If you are going to do the good work of celebrating the liturgy with each grade level, make it count. Keep upgrading their participation in hearing the word and in singing their praise. To the best of their abilities, let them in on the preparations, including the choice of readings.

The purpose of this "upgrading" isn't to have better school Masses. The Introduction to the children's lectionary (9) says that "children are always to be led to the parish's Sunday celebration of the eucharist." In other words, the liturgy is something to grow into, not to grow out of.

We have an all-school Mass on the first Friday of each month. Sometimes the Friday happens to fall on a special feast day, but most times it's just an ordinary day. I'm not very satisfied with this arrangement.

The year has its plain and simple weeks as well as its festive, crowded ones. The liturgy schedule can take this into account. It's best if a school plans the year's schedule of Masses to take advantage of the church's calendar. That's a lot more satisfying than sticking to "Mass every Friday" or some other rigid arrangement.

The Introduction to the *Lectionary for Masses with Children* (25) says that the keeping of the church's calendar "is vital to Catholic identity." Seasons and festival days can have great appeal for children — an appeal that, if fostered now, can last them all their lives.

Yes, keeping the church's year may mean a bit more juggling of schedules, but you will have opened up for students much of the joy and challenge of being a Roman Catholic.

What would you give priority in scheduling weekday Masses with children?

First, you probably want to schedule liturgies for Advent and Lent and Eastertime, not in celebration of a saint's day but in celebration of the season itself. It's also good to schedule a liturgy for the week after Christmas break so the students can celebrate at least the final days of Christmastime together.

Second, especially if the holy days of obligation are school days, you may need to schedule Mass for these: November 1, All Saints; December 8, the Immaculate Conception; and Ascension Day, the 40th day of Eastertime. The Immaculate Conception would be one of the Advent liturgies of the year, and the Ascension would be one of the Eastertime liturgies.

During Ordinary Time, you might make a point to choose some of the other church festivals for your days of celebration — for instance, Holy Cross, All Souls and Candlemas, as well as a few saints' days. And of course you will want a big celebration for your patronal day.

What is a patronal day?

If you are in the parish of St. John Bosco, January 31 is your own solemnity. No matter what the rank of the day on the calendar, in your parish your patronal day is raised to the rank of solemnity.

Perhaps your parish is not named after a saint. You still have your "titular solemnity," the day that corresponds to your parish title. For instance, Ascension School would make the most of the solemnity of the Ascension of the Lord.

Sometimes it takes some searching in old church calendars or other resources to find when a parish day is observed. If it always falls on a Sunday or during Lent or during school vacation, you might consider seeking out an alternative date to keep each year.

For example, St. John the Baptist is remembered on June 24 (his birth) and August 29 (his martyrdom). Instead of missing out because these days fall during summer, perhaps the parish school of St. John the Baptist can celebrate their patron every Advent or on the day after the feast of the Baptism of the Lord.

Most children love holidays and so do I. Which ones are best to celebrate and what are some good ways to do this?

The principal days that can fall on a weekday during the school year are not many:

September 14,	The Holy Cross
*November 1,	All Saints
November 2,	The Commemoration of All the Faithful Departed (All Souls)
November 9,	The Dedication of the Lateran Basilica
*December 8,	The Immaculate Conception of Mary (an Advent celebration)
February 2,	The Presentation of the Lord
Ash Wednesday,	the beginning of the lenten fast
March 19,	St. Joseph, the Husband of Mary (most always in Lent)
March 25,	The Annunciation of the Lord (most always in Lent)
First 8 days of Easter,	The Easter Octave (a full week of solemnities!)
*40th day of Easter,	The Ascension of the Lord
	**a holy day of obligation*

Also, there's your parish solemnity. And you'll want to add to this list several of the saints' days — perhaps Michael, Gabriel and Raphael, or Francis of Assisi, or Cecilia, or Nicholas, or Lucy, or Elizabeth Ann Seton.

In celebration of festival days, we can begin by preparing a splendid liturgy. Especially if a day isn't a holy day of obligation, when Mass is required, you really should consider celebrating Morning or Midday Prayer with children. These are lively liturgies of psalms and hymns.

A well-kept liturgy is a tall order in itself, but sacred days ask a bit more of us. Perhaps there's also a fancy lunch menu, an afternoon party with games, a dress-up day in keeping with the celebration.

Schools have their own annual events — "Citizenship Day," "International Day," "Self-Esteem Day," and the like. A parochial school might skip some of this, but borrow the ideas and use them in celebration of a church festival. For instance, an international smorgasbord might be a great way to celebrate All Saints.

Festivals take preparation during the days or even weeks beforehand. Perhaps there are scriptures or lives of the saints to research, art projects to put together, holiday songs to rehearse, or blessings and folk customs to organize.

The *Leader's Manual* of the *Hymnal for Catholic Students* has a very fine and thorough section about keeping several of the church festivals in school. There are suggestions for Mass or a prayer service and ideas for other ways to keep the days.

At Mass, sometimes we dramatize the gospel reading, or we have a student dress up as one of the saints we're celebrating. What are good ways to do these things?

Dramatizing the scriptures and having a "visit" by a saint can be a wonderful way to celebrate a special day — but not at Mass. The Introduction to the *Lectionary for Masses with Children* (52) is fairly blunt about not having plays or costumes at Mass:

> *The Mass is not a historical reenactment of the events of salvation history and care should be taken not to give the impression that the liturgy of the word is a play.*

The liturgy is not about the "long ago and far away." Through the scriptures we proclaim, through the psalms we sing, through our thanksgiving around the altar, the past, present and future become God's timeless "now."

Is that too amazing to imagine? And yet that's what we sing at Mass when we join with the angels in singing God's praise.

There are customary ways to proclaim the scriptures at Mass that prompt interest and help to build enthusiasm. Sometimes a reading is divided up among different readers. Readers can wear albs, which are the right vestment for anyone who is baptized. Banners, incense and candles are used to make the reading of the gospel more festive.

You might ask yourself if the lectionary is beautiful, if the reader is dressed well and has good physical presence, if the gospel procession and other movement and singing involved in the liturgy of the word are everything they can be.

The *Directory for Masses with Children* (47) offers a suggestion for saints' days:

The interpretation and explanation of the readings from the scriptures in the Mass on a saint's day may include an account of the saint's life, not only in the homily but even before the readings, in the form of an introduction.

LTP's *Companion to the Calendar* includes brief accounts of the lives of the saints that may be perfect for this purpose.

I notice that each set of weekday readings has a theme printed on top, such as "Love everyone." What's the purpose of these themes?

Those words can help us locate or relocate a set of readings when we make choices from among the many sets of readings.

Individual readings also have a line or two for much the same purpose. Hardly anybody knows offhand what Matthew 6:25 – 33 is about. But add the line "Do not worry about tomorrow," as the lectionary does, and, without reading the whole passage again, we may be able to recollect that the reading is Jesus' lesson about the lilies of the field.

Of course, this gospel passage is about a lot more than not worrying. It's also about trust, about God's continual care, about sacrificing everything for the sake of the kingdom of heaven. A person could probably write a book about the passage.

In any case, we do not prepare liturgy around a theme. We wouldn't reduce a fine piece of music or a beautiful poem to a few notes or a few words. Why do that with the paschal mystery?

The scriptures and songs for Mass should not be chosen in order to get across a message. They're chosen in celebration of Christ. The Introduction to the children's lectionary (24) reminds us of this mystery:

The liturgy of the word is neither a catechetical session nor an introduction to biblical history. The liturgy celebrates the word of God in narrative and song, makes it visible in gesture and symbol, and culminates in the celebration of the eucharist.

The school uses the children's lectionary for the weekly school eucharist. A number of parishioners join us. Some of them are asking why we don't use the weekday readings from the regular lectionary. What do I tell them?

At daily Mass, from day to day the church reads gradually through books of the Bible. This is called *lectio continua,* consecutive reading. The greatest benefit here is for those who go to Mass every day.

The weekday volume of the *Lectionary for Masses with Children* was designed not for daily Mass but for weekly or occasional celebrations, so the readings are not organized according to a *lectio continua.*

Of course, everyone would be welcome to a school Mass. Many daily churchgoers take special delight in Masses with children. But they shouldn't expect to hear the readings for daily Mass any more than they should expect those readings at a funeral or at a wedding. That might need a few words of explanation. Also, the school Mass probably shouldn't be timed to replace a regularly scheduled weekday Mass, although in some parishes this may be unavoidable.

If a feast or other occasion (such as Mass with children) interrupts the consecutive readings at daily Mass, the presider is permitted to add the passage to the reading the day before or the day after the interruption.

Walk me quickly through the liturgical year.

Let's start in spring, when the world seems reborn:

Lent lasts from Ash Wednesday to Holy Thursday. Notice that Lent ends on Holy Thursday, not Holy Saturday. Lent is a preparation not for Easter Sunday but for the Paschal Triduum. Lent is the church's time to get back to basics — to prayer, simple living and charity. Perhaps the most basic of these basics is faithfulness to the promises we made at baptism.

From Holy Thursday evening until Easter Sunday evening is the Paschal Triduum, which means the "three days of Passover." In the death, burial and resurrection of the Lord, the church "passes over." Baptism, confirmation and eucharist are the paschal sacraments. Every Roman Catholic is asked to put everything else aside to keep these holiest of holy days.

The Easter season is the 50 days from Easter Sunday to Pentecost. (On Easter Sunday, the Triduum and Eastertime overlap.) Eastertime is Lent's "alter ego." Lent is a fast; Eastertime is a feast. Together, Lent, Triduum and Eastertime make up a quarter of the year, the springtime of the church.

After Pentecost is a long stretch of Ordinary Time, almost half the year. Ordinary Time really isn't a church season, just a term to help describe the weeks in between seasons. (Here the word "ordinary," like the word "ordinal," means "counted," not "plain." The weeks are counted especially to help us organize the lectionary.)

Eventually autumn dwindles down and the days are as short as they can get. We keep Advent, which begins four Sundays before Christmas and lasts until Christmas Eve, when the season of Christmas begins.

At Christmas the days ever-so-slowly begin to lengthen; they'll keep on lengthening through the winter and on into spring. Christmastime lasts until the feast of the Baptism of the Lord, which in most years falls on the Sunday after Epiphany. Advent and Christmastime balance each other. First we make ready and then we celebrate the coming of Christ.

Between the feast of the Baptism and Ash Wednesday is Ordinary Time again. We count the winter weeks to another Lent. No matter what season it is, the church is always celebrating the paschal mystery — Christ in our flesh and blood, Christ who died for our sake, Christ in glory, Christ who sends us the Spirit.

Each week we also celebrate the paschal mystery: We fast in repentance on Fridays and feast in thanksgiving on Sundays. Each year in spring we keep one unique Friday and Saturday and Sunday with all our might — and that's another way to describe the Paschal Triduum.

Every day we celebrate the paschal mystery, especially during the two "passovers" of the day, when the sun rises and when it sets. That's one reason why Morning and Evening Prayer are liturgies of the church.

On some days we have a feast and we hear a particular gospel. On some days we remember a particular saint. On all these days the stories and remembrances may change, but the mystery is the same, and this mystery is Christ.

Guidelines

For Selecting Readings from the Lectionary for Masses with Children

For Masses with children, you may choose readings from the regular lectionary or from the children's lectionary.

Note that the children's lectionary does not have readings for Holy Thursday, Good Friday or the Easter Vigil. On these days you must use the regular lectionary.

At parish Masses on Christmas Day, Epiphany, the Sundays of Lent, Easter Sunday, Ascension Day, and Pentecost, the children's lectionary may be used only when the liturgy of the word is celebrated with children in a place apart from the main assembly.

To select readings from the children's lectionary, you need to know the liturgical title and rank (if any) of the day on which you will be celebrating Mass. You also need to know what season the day falls in. This information is found in the year's liturgical calendar (sometimes called an "ordo").

Note that some saints' days are optional. If you are not observing an optional day, follow the guidelines below for a "weekday that is not a saint's day, solemnity or feast."

A liturgical calendar may or may not include the parish's patronal solemnity. When is it? (See page 23 for more about this celebration.)

For sacramental celebrations, such as communal reconciliation or first communion, use the readings for the sacraments, which are found in the weekday volume of the children's lectionary; or you may use appropriate readings from the seasonal sections of the weekday volume.

On All Sundays Throughout the Year

Use the readings for the Sunday, found in the appropriate Sunday volume, Year A, B or C. (The year's liturgical calendar will tell you what letter the year is.)

On Weekdays in Ordinary Time

If it is a solemnity or feast or November 2 (All Souls' Day): Use the day's readings, found in the Proper of Saints in the weekday volume.

On some days the Proper of Saints will direct you to choose from certain options in the Common sections.

Readings (#164 – 166) for the solemnity of the Sacred Heart of Jesus (the third Friday after Pentecost) are found in the appropriate Sunday volume, Year A, B or C.

If it is a saint's day that is not a solemnity or feast:

- Choose from the options for the day as directed by the Proper of Saints.
- Or choose from the weekday readings for Ordinary Time, #193 – 231. (#228 – 231 are especially for November.)
- Or choose from the readings "for various needs and occasions," #492 – 535.

If it is a weekday that is not a saint's day, solemnity or feast:

- Choose from the weekday readings for Ordinary Time, #193 – 231. (#228 – 231 are especially for November.)
- Or choose from the readings "for various needs and occasions," #492 – 535.

On Weekdays in Advent, Lent or Eastertime

If it is a solemnity or feast:

Use the day's readings, found in the Proper of Saints in the weekday volume.

On some days the Proper of Saints will direct you to choose from certain options in the Common sections.

The first eight days of Eastertime (the Easter Octave) are solemnities, but the children's lectionary does not have specific readings for the weekdays of the Octave. Readings #185 in the Eastertime section of the weekday volume are appropriate for these days.

The readings (#52 – 54) for the solemnity of the Ascension of the Lord (always a Thursday, the 40th day of Eastertime) are found in the appropriate Sunday volume, Year A, B or C.

If it is a saint's day that is not a solemnity or feast:

- Choose from the weekday readings of the season: Advent, #172 – 175; Lent, #176 – 184; Eastertime, #185 – 192. (These sections are a good source of readings even on saints' days.)
- Or choose from the options for the day as directed by the Proper of Saints.
- Or combine readings from the seasonal section and from the Proper of Saints: For instance, choose a first reading from the seasonal section and a gospel from the readings for the saint, or vice versa.

If it is a weekday that is not a saint's day, solemnity or feast:

- Choose from the weekday readings of the season: Advent, #172 – 175; Lent, #176 – 184; Eastertime, #185 – 192.

On Weekdays in Christmastime

If it is a solemnity or feast:

Use the day's readings, found in the Sunday volumes or in the Proper of Saints in the weekday volume.

Readings for the Birth of the Lord (Christmas Day), the Holy Family, Mary the Mother of God, and the Baptism of the Lord are found in the appropriate Sunday volume, Year A, B or C.

One reading each for the feasts of St. Stephen (#437), St. John (#438) and the Holy Innocents (#439) is found in the Proper of Saints in the weekday volume. You might pair this reading with one of those suggested on page 59 in this guide.

If it is a weekday that is not a solemnity or feast:

- There is no section for Christmastime in the weekday volume of the children's lectionary. See the suggestions on page 59 in this guide.

Suggestions *for* Weekday Masses *with* Children

In this section we divided the school year roughly into two-week blocks. For each block we suggest Mass readings, psalm refrains and hymns, and we offer sample intercessions. We also share some thoughts about feasts and saints' days that fall within each block of time; these are discussed in the context of the natural progression of the school year.

When we suggest a reading, we're not saying that it's the best choice. We're simply saying that it seems to be appropriate to the time of year. Anyone versed in the liturgy could survey the options and come up with a different list of appropriate suggestions.

These suggestions were given to fire imaginations and to open up possibilities, but not to give "recipes." There still are choices to be made, but we have narrowed them down a bit to help the time-strapped folks who prepare weekday Mass with children.

In making these suggestions, the most important consideration was the season of the year, with its traditional scriptures, melodies, poetry, customs and motifs. A Christian poet spoke of the liturgical year as the wedding ring we wear as a reminder of our loving fidelity to Christ.

We Christians use the signs of the seasons to celebrate the paschal mystery — the mystery of the Lord's incarnation, death, burial, resurrection and of the Lord's gift of the Spirit to the church. The paschal mystery is the "theme" of every liturgy. While the seasons change, the mystery remains the same.

The Introduction to the *Lectionary for Masses with Children* (26) reminds us:

> *Each day Christ's church is dying and coming to new life in him through the indwelling of the Spirit given at baptism. In ritual prayer, past and future are caught up into God's eternal present.*

Our suggestions for readings, psalms and songs were not made to help the liturgy make a point or stress some particular teaching. The liturgy is an entrance into eternity, an encounter with Christ. That's what all of us can come to expect in hearing the word and in offering our praise.

Suggested First Readings and Gospels for Weekdays

Except on solemnities, Mass on a weekday usually has two readings: a reading from one of the four gospels and a first reading from one of the other books of the Bible. At Masses with children, the liturgy of the word may include a first reading and a gospel reading, or simply a gospel reading. (See the *Directory for Masses with Children,* 42.)

The suggested readings were chosen from the weekday volume of the *Lectionary for Masses with Children.* For each block of weeks, two or three suggestions are given for a first reading and a gospel.

Readings usually were chosen from the appropriate seasonal section, for instance, the "Season of Advent" or "Ordinary Time." Occasionally there are suggestions from elsewhere in the lectionary, such as the "Masses for Various Needs and Occasions." For example, readings "For Unity of Christians" are suggested in January.

Psalm Refrains

The psalms are songs of Israel and songs of the church. Teaching psalm-singing to children offers them an enormous gift, a gift that is their birthright as Christians.

For each set of readings, the *Lectionary for Masses with Children* provides a psalm. This psalm or any other psalm that shares its spirit (as long as it's really a psalm) is sung between the readings. If there's only one reading at Mass, the psalm can be sung after the homily (see the *Directory for Masses with Children,* 46).

Psalms also can be sung as the opening song, at the preparation of the gifts and during the communion procession. For Roman Catholics it's traditional to sing psalms instead of hymns at the opening of Mass and during communion.

Psalms often are sung "responsorially." This means that a cantor sings the verses (or a reader reads them) and everyone responds by singing a refrain. The psalm refrains suggested here for weekdays were chosen from those in GIA/LTP's *Hymnal for Catholic Students.*

Repeating the same psalm over a number of weeks (instead of singing a different one at every Mass) can help us learn it by heart. In this way the psalm becomes our property, a song we can sing at other times in our lives. A seasonal psalm — the same psalm repeated at every liturgical celebration throughout a season — becomes a "theme song" of the church year.

The translation of the psalms in the *Lectionary for Masses with Children* is unique to that book. Music is being published for these psalms, but do children really need their own private psalms? The psalms and their melodies are a treasury that adults and children deserve to own together.

If the parish has a Sunday repertory of music for the psalms, it makes sense to sing these psalms at weekday Mass. (Notice that the psalm refrains in the children's lectionary often match many refrains already familiar to parishes that sing the psalms.) If the weekday music matches as much as possible what's sung on Sundays, children will be better able to energize the Sunday assembly.

Suggested Hymns

Hymns were selected from GIA/LTP's *Hymnal for Catholic Students.* Even if other songbooks are used with children, the suggestions here can spark ideas.

Singing the liturgy is traditional for Roman Catholics. The *Lectionary for Masses with Children* (51) reminds us once again that "the eucharistic liturgy requires the full use of music." That statement might present a special challenge to budgetary priorities.

Hymns are just one way we sing the liturgy. There also are psalms, litanies, acclamations and other chants. It's important to sing the parts of Mass that stay mostly the same from week to week — for instance, the alleluias, the amens, the "Holy, holy, holy," the memorial acclamation, and the "Lamb of God."

There's no reason for the melodies to change much through the year. Hymns and psalms are suggested in this book because they tend to change most from season to season. Someone will need to select a few to teach each year.

Repetition is a way to learn music. It can take many encounters with a new melody before it grows familiar enough to become prayer. Repetition is valuable week by week, but it's especially needed year by year: Sing the same tunes every Advent and they likely will be more and more welcome each year they return.

Ordinarily a weekday Mass has an opening psalm or hymn and maybe (but not always) a closing hymn. The preparation of the gifts is often a good time for a brief piece by a chorus, a few student instrumentalists or a solo.

Communal singing and the communion procession clearly belong together. The psalm or song at communion can stay the same at every Mass throughout a season or span of weeks. Something gentle and flowing works well with a procession, such as "Blest are they," "Eat this bread," "Gift of finest wheat," "I received the living God," "Jesu, Jesu," "Now we remain," or "Ubi Caritas."

Psalm 23, "My shepherd is the Lord," and Psalm 34, "Taste and see the goodness of the Lord," are especially traditional for the communion procession.

Sample Intercessions

In the intercessions we place before God the needs of the church and of the world, and our own needs as well. The presider introduces them; when they are over, the presider offers a prayer to God, and we answer "Amen."

Intercessions go together to form a litany. The *Lectionary for Masses with Children* (51) includes a special plea for singing them. Litanies usually work best if petitions are short and numerous, with an even back-and-forth between the person singing the petitions and everyone's response — like the litany of the saints.

The sample intercessions we give are brief. We call them "samples" because the intercessions you actually use will need to be composed with an open ear to the events of the news and the needs of your own community: "For the people of Bosnia, we pray to the Lord." "For Sharon Baker's mother, who is sick, . . ." "For good judgment in our student council elections, . . ." "For the prayers we hold in our hearts, . . ."

Autumn Ordinary Time

ENDS THE DAY BEFORE ADVENT BEGINS

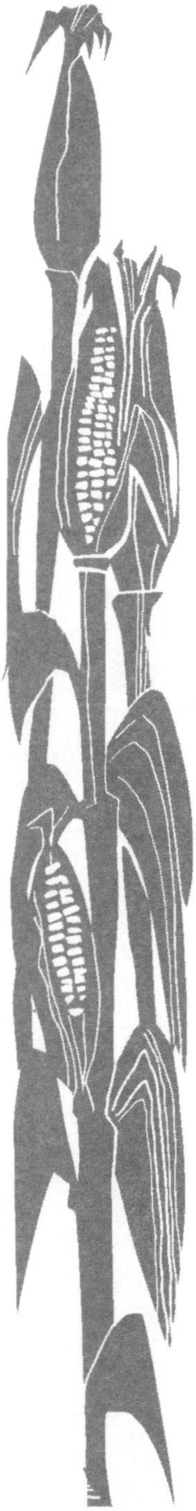

Especially in September's feast of the angels and in November's solemnity of the saints, throughout these weeks the church celebrates the harvest. It's not just farmers who are "bringing in the sheaves," but Christ as well, the Lord of the harvest, who will gather creation into heaven.

In the *Lectionary for Masses with Children,* notice that the final sets of weekday readings for Ordinary Time (#228 – 231) are marked "last weeks in Ordinary Time." These scriptures fit the flavor of November; they speak of the coming of the kingdom of heaven.

As autumn draws near to Advent, the liturgy speaks often of going home to heaven. Death and the life of the world to come are not subjects to avoid. The entertainment industry bombards us with endless exploitive and hideous images of death; religious educators have an obligation to deal with this subject in an honest, wholesome and Christian manner.

Earlier in autumn, as the academic year is off and running, God's word can instruct us in the ways of kindness and appreciation. We may need the scripture's good advice to encourage us to use our gifts for the benefit of one another. The readings, psalms and songs for this time are well-matched to the inauguration of the student council and other "beginnings" of the academic year.

The suggested readings for weekday Masses with children often revolve around images of God's protection and our responsibility to care for one another. There's a strong emphasis on hospitality and on love of neighbor. In the gospel readings, Jesus urges us to recognize that the kingdom of God is here among us.

This is a time of year to begin food and clothing drives. It's excellent to bring gifts to Mass for those who are needy and to collect them when the bread and wine are brought up. Gifts can go into a big hamper; a good place to keep them during Mass is in the main aisle rather than right in front of the altar. (It's never appropriate to put things in between the altar and the people, and that includes decorations.)

Classroom decorations can be used to help students keep the church year. Don't teach students a card-store kind of year, where the Halloween decorations go up on the first of October and come down on the first of November. Instead, in the classroom, why not match the decorations to the church festivals?

That might mean pumpkins and scarecrows and autumn leaves in October, with spooky Halloween decorations added a few days before the end of the month. Then they're in place for the celebration of All Saints and All Souls, when we begin the November-long remembrance of our holy ancestors.

In November the spooky images gradually can be replaced by Thanksgiving cornucopias and turkeys. Then, when Advent arrives, all the accumulated autumn finery can come down like leaves falling off a tree.

SEPTEMBER 1 TO SEPTEMBER 15

ORDINARY TIME

The *Lectionary for Masses with Children,* #492, includes readings for a Mass or liturgy of the word at the beginning of the school year, although these do not need to be used. It might be good to have the first Mass on one of the beautiful feast days that fall at this time of year; these days have their own readings.

September 8 is the feast of the Birth of the Virgin Mary. A suggested first reading is #448-2 from the Common of the Blessed Virgin Mary, Ephesians 1:3 – 6, "Christ chose us." A suggested gospel is #175, Luke 1:46 – 56, Mary's song of praise.

September 14 is the feast of the Holy Cross. With the sign of the cross we can dedicate the year. Readings for the feast are found under September 14 in the Proper of Saints, #370. On this day, some places venerate the cross in the way this is done on Good Friday. The classroom crucifix can be decorated with flowers.

There's rarely much time to prepare the first liturgies of the school year, which is all the more reason to develop a sound tradition and then stick to it year after year.

Catechetical Sunday always falls in September. Many parishes plan weekday celebrations, too. For an information packet call Publications Services of the United States Catholic Conference, 1-800-235-8722. (Materials become available the previous spring.)

Readings

#195:

1 Timothy 2:1 – 4, *"I ask you to pray for everyone."*
Matthew 6:7 – 13, *"You should pray like this: Our Father . . ."*

Or #202:

1 Peter 4:10 – 11, *"Each of you are blessed with God's gifts."*
Matthew 25:14 – 29, *"Because you were reliable in small matters, I will put you in charge of much more."*

Or #207:

Isaiah 41:10, *"Don't be afraid! I am with you."*
Mark 10:13 – 16, *"Let the children come to me."*

Psalm Refrain

Psalm 33, *"Happy the people the Lord has chosen."*
Or Psalm 34, *"Taste and see the goodness of the Lord."*

Hymns

"Bring forth the kingdom" *(works well with a cantor, but can be sung without one)*
"Eat this bread" *(like Psalm 34, a communion song)*
"Gather us in"
"Lord of all hopefulness" *(a lilting Irish tune)*
"Lift high the cross" *(perfect for September 14 and through the month)*

Sample Intercessions

For a bright new beginning to the school year . . .
For students and their families . . .
For teachers and principals . . .
For loving kindness and gentleness in this new year . . .
For patience and cooperation . . .

SEPTEMBER 16 TO SEPTEMBER 30

ORDINARY TIME

St. Matthew's feast comes on the 21st. A suggested first reading is #452-2 from the Common of Apostles, Ephesians 2:20 – 22, "The apostles are your foundation." The gospel for the feast is #376, Matthew 9:9 – 13, about Jesus calling Matthew to be a disciple.

September 29 is a wonderful day, the feast of the archangels Michael, Gabriel and Raphael. The readings for the day (#381) are found under September 29 in the Proper of Saints. Give this feast first consideration if you plan to celebrate Mass with children during these weeks.

A few days later, on October 2, we keep the memorial of the guardian angels. On these angels' days, we welcome the autumn and ask for God's guidance in the growing darkness. It's not hard to find pictures and statues and other images of angels to mix with the autumn decorations in the classroom.

Interestingly, the word "angel" is Greek for "messenger." Even John the Baptist was called an angel. (In art he's sometimes shown with wings!) Maybe anyone who spreads the good news is an angel.

Throughout these days it seems right to hear from Matthew's gospel. The festival of the angels suggests readings about God's guardianship. With the school year under way, everyone needs a dose of encouragement in cooperation and generosity. The suggested readings for weekday Mass may help in this.

Readings

#194:

1 Corinthians 13:4 – 7, *"Love is kind and patient."*
Matthew 5:43 – 48, *"Love your enemies."*

Or #198:

Colossians 3:12 – 13, *"Forgive anyone who does you wrong."*
Matthew 7:1 – 5, *"God will treat you as you treat others."*

Or #227:

1 John 3:1, 23, *"God wants us to love each other."*
John 15:12 – 15, *"Love each other as I have loved you."*

Psalm Refrain

Psalm 34, *"Taste and see the goodness of the Lord."*
Or Psalm 138, *"In the sight of the angels, I will sing your praises, Lord."*

Hymns

"All things bright and beautiful"
"For the beauty of the earth"
"Ye watchers and ye holy ones" *("Watchers" is another word for "angels"; this song can be learned now and sung again on All Saints.)*

Sample Intercessions

For peace and safety in this autumn season . . .
For the courage to do what is right . . .
For humility and kindness . . .
For all who love and care for us . . .
For our friends and enemies alike . . .

OCTOBER 1 TO OCTOBER 15
ORDINARY TIME

After all the fresh starts of September, October is a month of settling into the year's work.

Harvest time is here, and almost everywhere the autumn is coming on strong. The change of seasons can be a fine occasion for praising God for the goodness of creation and for giving thanks for God's gifts. Chilly weather can help renew concern for those in need of good food, warm clothing and housing.

Consider celebrating with children the memorials of Therese of the Child Jesus, who's also known as "the Little Flower" (October 1), of the Guardian Angels (October 2), of Francis of Assisi (October 4, a day when many parishes hold a blessing of animals), or of Teresa of Jesus (October 15).

See chapter 25 in the *Book of Blessings* and page 174 in *Catholic Household Blessings and Prayers* for help in organizing a blessing of animals.

The suggested readings for these weeks were chosen in the spirit of these saints: We can take delight in simple things and live less wastefully, more in harmony with the good earth. We can learn to share the gifts we have been given by God.

Readings

#196:

Colossians 3:1 – 2, *"Set your heart on heaven."*

Matthew 6:19 – 21, *"Your heart will be where your treasure is."*

Or #205:

Isaiah 30:19 – 20, 23 – 24, 26, *"The Lord is your teacher."*

Mark 5:21 – 24, 35 – 36, 38 – 42, *the raising of Jairus' daughter*

Or #228:

James 2:14 – 17, *"Show your faith by doing good deeds."*

Matthew 7:21, 24 – 27, *"Anyone who obeys my teachings is like a wise person who builds a house on solid rock."*

Psalm Refrain

Psalm 138, *"In the sight of the angels, I will sing your praises, Lord."*

Or Psalm 15, *"Those who do justice will live in the presence of the Lord."*

Hymns

"All creatures of our God and king" *(based on some words by St. Francis)*

"Earth and all stars"

"Let all things now living" *(a Welsh folk song that can be learned now and sung again at Thanksgiving)*

"Sing out, earth and skies" *(almost a dance!)*

Sample Intercessions

For the health of the world and its peoples . . .

For everyone who cares for the earth and its creatures . . .

For those who need help as the weather grows cold . . .

For farmers who bring in the harvest . . .

For all who show us the way to heaven . . .

OCTOBER 16 TO OCTOBER 30
ORDINARY TIME

On the last weekend of the month, in most places, clocks are moved back an hour, which can really bring home how long the nights have become. Halloween decorations can be a way to laugh at our fear of the dark. In Christ, we will have the last laugh over the long night of death.

The memorial of the North American martyrs (October 19), coming soon after Columbus Day, can be a time to celebrate Native American culture. Reading #457-2, from the Common of Martyrs (2 Corinthians 6:4 – 10, "We seem to be dying, and yet we are still alive"), makes an excellent first reading.

The feasts of the gospel writer Luke (October 18) and of the apostles Simon and Jude (October 28) can prepare us for the solemnity of all the saints. Gospel #455-2 from the Common of Apostles, Luke 6:12 – 16, lists all twelve apostles by name.

The suggested weekday readings speak of self-offering, about taking a risk to love others, about getting another chance when we fail. It's appropriate to hear from Luke's gospel during these weeks, and with All Saints so close, hymns about the martyrs and apostles seem right.

Readings

#211:

Isaiah 43:1 – 3, 5, *"Don't be afraid."*

Luke 7:11 – 17, *the raising of the widow's son*

Or #214:

1 John 3:11, 18, *"Show your love by helping others."*

Luke 10:25 – 37, *the Good Samaritan*

Or #216:

Colossians 2:6 – 7, *"Plant your roots in Christ."*

Luke 13:6 – 9, *"I'll make my fig tree grow."*

or gospel #396 (from October 18, St. Luke's Day):

Luke 10:1 – 9, *"Ask the Lord of the harvest to send out workers."*

Psalm Refrain

Psalm 15, *"Those who do justice will live in the presence of the Lord."*

Or Psalm 84, *"How lovely is your dwelling place, O Lord of hosts."*

Hymns

"All hail the pow'r of Jesus' name" *(a fine American folk song for late autumn and for Advent)*

"Blessed feasts of blessed martyrs"

"Bring forth the kingdom"

"Let all on earth their voices raise" *(a song for the apostles, which mentions the dark night, that's fun to sing as a round)*

Sample Intercessions

For the bravery to live as Christians . . .

For people who risk their lives to help one another . . .

For nurses, doctors and all who heal the sick . . .

For a good harvest . . .

For a second chance when we fail . . .

OCTOBER 31 TO NOVEMBER 11

ORDINARY TIME

What a rich time of year! We remember the dead, we give thanks for the bounty of the earth, and we look forward to God's reign of justice. It's All Hallows' Tide. From the evening of October 31 through November 2 we keep a festival of heaven, and the celebration echoes throughout the month.

In the classroom and even in the ways you think about November, don't end Halloween too soon! Use its customs and decorations in celebration of the church's "days of the dead." Readings for All Saints are found on November 1 in the Proper of Saints, #402. For All Souls the readings "for the dead" would be chosen from #531 – 535.

In a handsome, blank-page book, students can write the names of the dead. The book can be kept in a place of honor in the classroom throughout the month. On All Souls or some other time this month, during the intercessions at eucharist or a liturgy of the word, mention aloud these names.

The Lateran Basilica is the cathedral of Rome. The anniversary of its dedication is November 9. Like All Saints, the Dedication feast is a celebration of the new Jerusalem, where one day we will make our home. Readings for the day are chosen from the Common of the Dedication of a Church, #442 – 446, which also are appropriate throughout this time of year.

November 11 is "Martinmas," the memorial of St. Martin of Tours. He was a Roman soldier who became a Christian and a conscientious objector. Martin is a patron of peace. His day was chosen for the armistice that ended the First World War, which has become Veterans Day in the U.S.A. (In many other nations, today is a memorial day for those who died in war.)

Readings
#229:
Isaiah 25:6, 9, *"We have waited, and now God is here."*
Matthew 8:5 – 11, *"Many will enjoy the feast of heaven."*
Or #231:
Ephesians 3:16 – 17, 20 – 21, *"Christ's power is at work in us."*
Luke 17:20 – 21, *"God's kingdom is here with you."*
Or first reading #443 (from the common of the dedication of a church):
Ephesians 2:20 – 22, *"You are like a building with the saints as your foundation."*
with gospel #535-3 (from the Masses for the dead):
John 11:21 – 27, *"I am the one who raises the dead."*

Psalm Refrain
Psalm 84, *"How lovely is your dwelling place, O Lord of hosts."*
Or Psalm 122, *"We shall go up with joy to the house of our God."*

Hymns
"Blest are they" *(the beatitudes, a good communion song)*
"Come, ye thankful people, come" *(the perfect November hymn)*
"Sing with all the saints in glory"
"What wondrous love is this" *(a song of eternal life set to a haunting American folk tune)*

Sample Intercessions
For the church in heaven and on earth . . .
For people who have no place to call home . . .
For the sorrowful . . .
For the dead . . .
For all who are gathered here . . .

NOVEMBER 12 UNTIL ADVENT

Ordinary Time

These last days of Ordinary Time are much like Advent. We tell the scriptures of the end of the world, of judgment, of the banquet of heaven. As the weather outside grows worse, our thoughts turn inward. All nature seems to die, and we remember the dead; perhaps we may even dare to think about what lies beyond the grave.

In the United States, these are the days of our national harvest festival, Thanksgiving, which fits right into the church's keeping of November. This time of year gives us reasons to rejoice in our families and in God's blessed bounty, and it can rally our concern for those who need our help. Readings "For Productive Land and After the Harvest" (#518 – 522) seem to fit any weekday in November.

Many of the November saints were known for their work with the underprivileged or were poor themselves — Martin de Porres, Martin of Tours, Mother Cabrini, Margaret, Elizabeth, Rose Duchesne, Miguel Pro.

The suggested readings, psalms and songs match the generous spirit of these saints; the readings can work well for any weekday or saint's day celebration in November, including a pre-Thanksgiving liturgy, which may include gathering food and clothing for people in need.

Readings

#217:

James 2:14 – 18, *"Prove that you have faith by doing kind deeds."*

Luke 14:12 – 14, *"When you give a feast, invite the poor."*

Or #230:

Philippians 4:4 – 7, *"The Lord will soon be here."*

Luke 12:35 – 40, *"Be ready and keep your lamps burning."*

Or first reading #523 (for refugees and exiles):

Hebrews 13:1 – 3, 14 – 16, *"By welcoming guests, some have welcomed angels."*

with gospel #473-2 (from the common of saints):

Matthew 25:31 – 40, *"Come and receive the kingdom."*

Psalm Refrain

Psalm 24, *"Lord, this is the people that longs to see your face."*

Or Psalm 122, *"We shall go up with joy to the house of our God."*

Hymns

"Come, ye thankful people, come" *(a harvest hymn with beautiful images of Judgment Day)*

"For the beauty of the earth"

"Let all things now living"

"Now thank we all our God"

"Soon and very soon" *(a rousing spiritual for Advent as well)*

Sample Intercessions

That the hungry may be fed . . .

That the homeless may be sheltered . . .

That travelers will be safe . . .

That the dead may be raised . . .

That the kingdom of heaven may come soon . . .

Advent

FROM THE FOURTH SUNDAY BEFORE CHRISTMAS UNTIL CHRISTMAS EVE

Nights are as long as they get. The weather grows dreary. Travel can be difficult. Not that many years ago, this was the season that most stirred people's fears of starvation and disease and death. That's still true in some parts of the world. Advent can be a frightening time of year.

No wonder the Advent color is a somber purple, its melodies plaintive, its prayers filled with yearning! And no wonder the Advent scriptures are so filled with hope!

Advent reminds us of our need for a Savior, who comes with life and health and peace — and not only for ourselves but for all people in the world who are hungry or homeless, for all people who have been denied justice and freedom.

Children, too, have their fears — plenty of them. They see the trouble around them. Perhaps they are its victims. And children have their hopes and dreams. Advent can be the time of our most heartfelt prayers.

But Advent can be difficult to keep. Somehow, the days can get so stuffed with Christmas that there's not much room left for Advent, and that's a terrible loss. The school and religious education program can do their part in helping us to keep Advent by holding back on Christmas until it actually arrives. That's when to begin the celebration, which lasts well into January.

The first weeks of the new year are a time to hold an all-school Christmas Mass, but before Christmas the liturgy must remain an Advent one. Singing Christmas carols or proclaiming the Christmas gospels before Christmas Eve is antagonistic to our Catholic way of life.

Think positively about waiting for Christmas. For instance, instead of being red, white and green, classroom decorations for Advent can be a wintry purple, blue and silver. Instead of Christmas carols, Advent's songs can be sung. There are more than can be learned in a lifetime.

Advent has a rich array of customs — almost too many for this short season. There's the Advent wreath and Jesse tree and *Las Posadas.* There's St. Nicholas and St. Lucy, the Immaculate Conception and Our Lady of Guadalupe. And, of course, there are all the many preparations and rehearsals for Christmastime. Whew!

Save the tree and nativity scene until December 25 and the days that follow. Advent has plenty of its own customs, and, although the season is somber, the anticipation of what's to come is sweet.

THE FIRST SUNDAY OF ADVENT UNTIL DECEMBER 16

EARLY ADVENT

Now is our annual opportunity to immerse ourselves in a number of fascinating, intense and even scary subjects — death, judgment, heaven and hell. The Advent scriptures offer a prophetic vision of God's reign and a good context for discussing and celebrating these topics.

Happily, early Advent brings two celebrations of Mary: December 8 and 12, which can be kept with a mix of Marian and Advent songs. The Immaculate Conception is a holy day of obligation and the patronal day of the United States. Its readings are found on December 8 in the Proper of Saints, #429. Our Lady of Guadalupe is the patronal day of the Americas. An appropriate first reading is from the Common of the Blessed Virgin Mary, #447-2, Zechariah 2:14 – 15. A suggested gospel is #302 (also #352), Luke 1:39 – 56, the visit of Mary and Elizabeth.

For a blessing of an Advent wreath, see Chapter 47 in the *Book of Blessings.* An Advent wreath is more traditional (and more beautiful) when it is suspended on ribbons from the ceiling rather than being placed on a table. Regardless of its location, be sure to include at least a few real evergreen branches in your wreath.

Advent calendars are also customary in a classroom. LTP has published a beautiful one with tiny doors that are opened each day of the season.

December 1 is AIDS Awareness Day. The day is a reminder that when we talk about this disease we talk about family and friends and neighbors, and about ourselves, too. What do the scriptures and songs of this time of year have to say to our fears and hopes, to our living and our dying?

St. Nicholas, December 6, is the patron of children. St. Lucy, December 13, was herself a child when she was martyred. Advent scriptures and songs fit these beloved memorials perfectly. Each classroom might even have a "celestial visit" from St. Nicholas and St. Lucy.

Readings
There are four sets of weekday readings for Advent; the first three, #172 – 174, are appropriate for the days before December 17.

#172:
Isaiah 30:19 – 21, *"The Lord will not be hidden from you."*
Luke 12:35 – 38, *"Keep your lamps burning."*

Or #173:
Isaiah 30:19, 23 – 24, 26, *"The moon will be bright as the sun."*
Matthew 9:35 — 10:1, 5, 6 – 7, *"Announce that the kingdom of heaven will soon be here."*

Or #174:
Isaiah 40:25 – 26, 29 – 31, *"You will soar like an eagle."*
Luke 7:17 – 26, *"Go and tell John what you have seen."*

Psalm Refrain
Psalm 24, *"Lord, this is the people that longs to see your face."*
Or Psalm 25, *"To you, O Lord, I lift my soul."*

Hymns
"Freedom is coming" *(a song from South Africa)*
"I want to walk as a child of the light"
"Magnificat" *(the first words in Latin of Mary's song)*
"Prepare the way of the Lord" *(an Advent round)*
"Soon and very soon" *(a spiritual that can be sung quickly or slowly for two different moods)*

Sample Intercessions
For the day of the Lord to come soon . . .
For justice and fairness among nations . . .
For an end to quarrels and fighting . . .
For peace in our world and in our classrooms . . .
For patience as we wait for the Lord to come . . .

DECEMBER 17 UNTIL CHRISTMAS EVE
LATE ADVENT

The intensity of a child's anticipation of Christmas is very close to the mood of the liturgy during this final week of Advent.

A Mass before Christmas should never be a Christmas Mass. That would be hostile to the liturgy and to our Catholic tradition. Anyway, especially considering the beauty and richness of these days, why would anyone jump the gun on Christmas?

This final week of Advent has wonderful scriptures of its own, especially of the events that led to the birth of the Lord. From Luke we hear about angel Gabriel's annunciation to Zechariah and then to Mary, about Mary's visit to Elizabeth, about the birth of John. From Matthew we hear of Joseph's dream of an angel.

During this week it seems right to have a cleaning and decorating day to get classrooms ready for the festival. Then the decorations are in place when classes resume after the break, when there's still a number of days of the Christmas season to celebrate.

Readings
There are four sets of readings for weekdays in Advent. The final set, #175, is the best choice during the final week before Christmas:

2 Corinthians 1:3 – 4, *"God comforts us so we can share God's comfort with others."*
Luke 1:46 – 56, *Mary's song of praise, the Magnificat*

Or #316 (from the solemnity of the Birth of John the Baptist):
Jeremiah 1:4 – 8, *"I chose you before you were born."*
Luke 1:5 – 17, *Gabriel's appearance to Zechariah*

Or first reading #447-2 (from the common of the Blessed Virgin Mary):
Zechariah 2:14 – 15, *"I am coming to live with you."*
with gospel #302 (also #352):
Luke 1:39 – 56, *"When Elizabeth heard Mary's greeting, the baby moved within her."*

Psalm Refrain
Psalm 25, *"To you, O Lord, I lift my soul."*
Or Psalm 27, *"The Lord is my light and my salvation."*

Hymns
See the other suggestions for Advent on page 53.

By tradition, the hymn "O come, O come, Emmanuel" is special to the final days of Advent. It is a hymn version of the "O antiphons" sung at Evening Prayer from December 17 to 23. That's why the hymn has seven verses, one for each evening of this week.

Sample Intercessions
For the children throughout the world . . .
For those who try to bring comfort and joy to others . . .
For peacemakers . . .
For parents expecting a new baby . . .
For anyone waiting for something wonderful to happen . . .

Christmastime

THE BIRTH OF THE LORD UNTIL THE BAPTISM OF THE LORD

The church doesn't call Christmas "Jesus' birthday." Christmas is not celebrated as the anniversary of Christ's birth. Instead, the church calls Christmas "the birth of the Lord." Amazing!

That means that we aren't celebrating something that happened long ago and far away. Christmas is a festival of something that happens here and now. And just like any birth, the birth of Christ comes with responsibilities — to feed, to clothe, to shelter Christ wherever our Lord is found. For unto us a child is born!

And so we try to invite everyone to share hospitality, to sing around the shining tree of life, to kiss and not to quarrel. Even the custom of gift-giving speaks of this "marvelous exchange": God is born human that humans might be born God.

Epiphany, which is kept in the United States on the first Sunday after January 1, is supposed to be the high point, not the end, of the Christmas season. Epiphany, after all, is the splendid festival when even a star shines out with the good news! Its light sparkles in the liturgy until February 2, the feast of the Presentation of the Lord.

Secular culture pretty well kicks Christmas out with the gift wrap on December 26. There's not much gained complaining about this, but recognize how inhuman the secular Christmas celebration can be. After months of advertising hype, the festival evaporates. That leaves all too many people, children included, feeling let down. We know we've been had!

The church calendar offers us a wholesome alternative — a Christmas season that we prepare in December and then celebrate in big and little ways for many days well into January.

Fortunately, this jolly season includes a few school days. And these few come when many of us need a dose of good cheer — in the first days of the new year, when winter often is at its worst.

The week after Epiphany has long been a time of half work and half play to help ease ourselves back into the routine. This is the perfect time for a Christmas Mass, as well as for classroom card and gift exchanges, for caroling and parties and pageants, for a visit from the Magi and for a blessing of the classroom or of the building itself in the new year.

(See Chapters 48 and 49 of the *Book of Blessings* for a blessing of the nativity scene and of a Christmas tree. See *Children's Daily Prayer* for a blessing of the classroom.)

THE BIRTH OF THE LORD UNTIL THE BAPTISM OF THE LORD
CHRISTMASTIME

The first Mass of the new year can be a Christmastime liturgy, another chance to sing carols and to hear the seasonal scriptures. That's really a wonderful way to kick off the second half of the academic year.

Notice how Christmastime has many solemnities and feasts. Each has its own readings and emphasis, but all these days are kept in celebration of Emmanuel, God with us. It's an important responsibility to keep the Christmas spirit bright throughout these weeks.

Several saints' days come during Christmastime, including a number of North Americans — Elizabeth Ann Seton (January 4), John Neumann (January 5) and André Bessette (January 6). Even the saints come clothed in Christmas cheer: On these days the songs and readings and prayers at Mass would best be about Christmas. The presider's collect at the end of the intercessions can be the opening prayer for the saint given in the sacramentary.

Readings
The weekday *Lectionary for Masses with Children* does not have a section for Christmastime, but elsewhere there are appropriate readings for a weekday Mass. The "season of Christmas" in the Sunday lectionary offers the familiar gospels of the birth of the Lord (#13, Luke 2:1 – 14) and of the visit of the Magi (#16, Matthew 2:1 – 12).

The second reading and gospel for the feast of the Holy Family would be a wonderful first reading and gospel for a weekday Mass with children. The readings are found in Years A, B or C of the Sunday lectionary, #14: Colossians 3:12 – 17, "Each one of you is part of the body of Christ," and Matthew 2:13 – 15, 19 – 23, about the flight into Egypt.

Or for a Christmastime weekday, consider the gospel story of the finding of the child Jesus in the Temple, Luke 2:41 – 51. This can be found in the weekday lectionary, #451-2, in the Common of the Blessed Virgin Mary. (It's also gospel #272 and 303.)

Psalm Refrain
Psalm 98 is traditional at Christmas; it begins, "Sing to the Lord a new song." "Joy to the world" is a carol version of this psalm that we all know.

Hymns
Carols, more carols and even more carols:
"Go tell it on the mountain"
"Joy to the world"
"O come, all ye faithful"
"Songs of thankfulness and praise"
"What child is this"

Sample Intercessions
For the church and all who love the church . . .
For our parish during these happy days . . .
For those who need the joy of Christmas . . .
For mothers and fathers, sisters and brothers . . .
For God's blessings in the new year . . .

Winter Ordinary Time
FROM CHRISTMASTIME UNTIL LENT

In the language of the church, Ordinary Time means "counted time," not "plain time." We count the weeks especially to help organize the lectionary. In winter, Ordinary Time begins on the day after the feast of the Baptism of the Lord and lasts until the day before Ash Wednesday.

The third Monday of January is the national day in celebration of the work of Dr. Martin Luther King, Jr. January 18 – 25 is the Church Unity Octave, a time of prayer for reconciliation and unity among the churches. And as we have discovered, much of our unity can be found in diversity. The Unity Octave ends on the feast of the Conversion of St. Paul.

During these weeks the brightest festival on the church calendar is February 2, the feast of the Presentation of the Lord, also called Candlemas, a wonderful day to bless candles and to march in procession in honor of Christ, the light of the world.

The day after is the memorial of St. Blase. Throats are blessed using Candlemas candles; this gesture is a prayer for health during the flu season. These days ordinarily come at the end of Catholic Schools Week, when several religious educators and church teachers have their memorials (Angela Merici, Thomas Aquinas, John Bosco).

Another popular holiday, St. Valentine's Day, usually falls during winter Ordinary Time, although in the years when Easter is early and February 14 comes soon after Ash Wednesday, the festivities can be low key, in keeping with the spirit of Lent.

In many places in the world, now is the "holiday season." These are the days to drive the cold winter away with singing and dancing, plays and musicals, puppetry and pantomime and all the human arts that bring cheer and delight.

The liturgy during these weeks echoes Epiphany. In January and February, as the days ever-so-slowly begin to lengthen, the church speaks often of light and healing and of God's gracious call to discipleship and unity.

Remember that Ash Wednesday can come as early as early February and as late as early March. So this winter span of Ordinary Time varies from one to two months long. Adapt the suggestions on pages 62 to 67 accordingly.

FROM THE DAY AFTER THE BAPTISM OF THE LORD
UNTIL JANUARY 26

ORDINARY TIME

Epiphany was such a "stellar" festival, its light still shines on these days of January. At Epiphany we heard of the gathering of all nations to worship the Lord. In January the church seems to explore ways that different groups of people can cooperate creatively.

The eight-day period ending on January 25, the feast of the Conversion of Paul (#247 in the Proper of Saints), is the Church Unity Octave. This once was celebrated with more vigor than it is now. Perhaps in years past people were better acquainted with the troubles resulting from ignorance and distrust of one another's ways.

Some religious educators organize a field trip to other denominations' churches for prayer and education. If you are hosting interdenominational prayer, a service of psalms or a liturgy of the word is appropriate.

The Martin Luther King holiday on the third Monday of the month is the nation's opportunity to remember and renew Dr. King's work for harmony among peoples. Readings in the weekday lectionary "for peace and justice" (#513 – 517) might be proclaimed at a liturgy of the word held in remembrance of the work of Dr. King.

Readings

#213:

Jeremiah 1:4 – 8, *"I chose you before you were born."*
Luke 9:1 – 6, *"The apostles went to tell the good news."*

Or #225:

1 Corinthians 12:12 – 13, *"God's Spirit made us part of Christ's body."*
John 15:1 – 5, *"I am the vine; you are the branches."*

Or first reading #509 (for the unity of Christians):

Ezekiel 36:24 – 28, *"I will bring you back home."*
with gospel #512-2:
Matthew 18:19 – 22, *"Whenever two or three come together in my name, I am there."*

Psalm Refrain

Psalm 98, *"All the ends of the earth have seen the power of God."*
Or Psalm 27, *"The Lord is my light and my salvation."*

Hymns

"In Christ there is no east or west" *(a song of Christian unity)*
"Earth and all stars"
"Shout for joy, loud and long" *(an old carol set to new words)*
"Sing a new song" *(like "Joy to the world," a metrical version of Psalm 98)*
"We shall overcome" *(an anthem of the civil rights movement)*

Sample Intercessions

For the churches of our city . . .
For church leaders . . .
For the people who teach us to live in peace . . .
For all people who want to live in freedom . . .
For all of us gathered here . . .

JANUARY 27 UNTIL A WEEK BEFORE ASH WEDNESDAY ORDINARY TIME

Catholic Schools Week begins at the end of January; it coincides with the memorials of several religious educators. For a packet of information, including suggestions for liturgy, write: National Marketing Campaign, National Catholic Education Association, 1077 30th Street NW, Washington DC 20007.

February 2 is the Presentation of the Lord, also called Candlemas. This splendid feast is a kind of turning point, offering a last look back to Christmas and a first glimpse of the paschal season. The readings of the feast are found in the lectionary on February 2 in the Proper of Saints, #252. Good ideas for Candlemas can be found in the *Leader's Manual* of the *Hymnal for Catholic Students,* beginning on page 78.

Some places make much of the blessing of throats on February 3, St. Blase's Day. (See Chapter 51 in the *Book of Blessings.*) It's strange how this old custom has survived the years. It comes from a time when just about every saint's day had some sort of special blessing. You might research these customs; a few might be right to add to other saints' day celebrations observed throughout the year.

Readings

#193:

Ephesians 5:8 – 10, *"Make your light shine."*

Matthew 5:14 – 16, *"You are like light for the world."*

Or #203:

Isaiah 55:10 – 11, *"My word does what I send it to do."*

or first reading #466-2 (from the common of pastors):

Ephesians 4:11 – 13, *"Christ chose us for different duties so his body would grow strong."*

Mark 4:1 – 9, *the parable of the sower*

Or #208:

Isaiah 42:16, *"I will give light to your paths."*

Mark 10:46 – 52, *the healing of Bartimaeus*

Psalm Refrain

Psalm 27, *"The Lord is my light and my salvation."*

Or Psalm 96, *"Bring an offering and enter his courts: in his temple worship the Lord."*

Hymns

Other suggestions for winter can be found on page 63.

"Bring forth the kingdom"

"This little light of mine"

"We are walking in the light"

"We see the Lord" *(a lively song, perfect for Candlemas)*

Sample Intercessions

That the light of heaven may shine in the church . . .

That the winter weather will not be dangerous . . .

That those who are sick may get well . . .

That we may grow strong in wisdom . . .

That we may be joyful in all we have been given . . .

THE WEEK BEFORE ASH WEDNESDAY
ORDINARY TIME

It's Carnival time! The merry feasting and fantasy of these days are a preparation for Lent's seriousness and simple living.

This time of year is famous for some of the most wonderful of the human arts — for puppetry, pantomime, masquerades and theatricals of all kinds. These arts can help us discover what it's like to walk around in someone else's shoes.

An amazing number of fairy tales, at least according to the original versions, take place during the days before Ash Wednesday, and sometimes the "big scene" happens at a Carnival dance. (Cinderella, "Ash Girl," is one of them.) Rediscover these stories. They are a delightful inheritance from our ancestors in the faith.

When St. Valentine's Day and the days of Carnival coincide, the two can coexist, joy upon joy. But when February 14 comes soon after Ash Wednesday, as it does in 1997, the celebration would be low-key. In any year, St. Valentine's Day would not be observed at Mass, although in the classroom a blessing of valentines (such as the one in LTP's *Children's Daily Prayer)* would be a fine way to christen the day.

Readings

#197:

Isaiah 46:4, *"I will take care of you."*

Matthew 6:25 – 33, *the lesson of lilies of the field*

#212:

1 John 4:7 – 10, *"We must love each other."*

Luke 7:36 – 50, *"The woman washed Jesus' feet with her tears."*

Or #215:

James 5:16 – 18, *"The prayer of an innocent person is powerful."*

Luke 11:5 – 10, *"Ask and you will receive."*

Psalm Refrain

Psalm 96, *"Bring an offering and enter his courts: in his temple worship the Lord."*

Or Psalm 34, *"Taste and see the goodness of the Lord."*

Hymns

Songs with plenty of alleluias can be sung to give this acclamation of praise a fond farewell before Lent arrives. Good ones are "All creatures of our God and king" and "Jubilate Deo," which is great to sing as a round. Other suggestions for winter are found on pages 63 and 65.

Sample Intercessions

For people who help us to see the world in new ways . . .
For musicians and artists and architects . . .
For dancers and actors . . .
For poets and writers . . .
For a good and holy Lent . . .

Lent

ASH WEDNESDAY UNTIL HOLY THURSDAY AFTERNOON

The word Lent comes from "lengthen." Days are growing longer. The advance of daylight can bring reassurance that goodness triumphs over evil — but not without a struggle.

The strengthening sun gives energy to winds. No wonder March is named after the god of war! Lent's blustery weather is an emblem for a Christian grappling with the wrongs of this world.

All that fresh air and sunshine gives the earth a spring cleaning. Many folks take this as a cue to clean out the cobwebs in their homes and in their brains.

Lent is a preparation for the Paschal Triduum, when the church baptizes. Getting ready to baptize others begs a question of those who are already baptized: How well have you been living up to those baptismal promises? That's why Lent is a season of repentance, a word that means "turning back." Lent brings us back to basics.

During Lent we renew the disciplines of prayer, fasting and almsgiving. Each Lent we Christians learn and relearn how to do these things with vigor and honesty. These are the basics that bring us back to the vows we made at baptism.

Prayer, fasting and almsgiving are old-fashioned words. Perhaps they even seem out-of-touch, but look again. What could be more in touch with the world? Simple living and sharing are just what the earth requires from its inhabitants.

In the poetry of the church, Lent leads us back to paradise, except now we refuse to eat. We won't make the same mistake twice. And Lent sets us aboard Noah's ark, where creation gets a second chance, where it's all for one and one for all.

Deliberately, there are very few saint's days during this season, and the few that are on the calendar are optional. Lent is too important to be interrupted too often. Three exceptions are the feast of the Chair of Peter, February 22, the solemnity of St. Joseph, usually March 19, and the solemnity of the Annunciation of the Lord, usually March 25.

In addition to saints' days, another thing the church "gives up" during Lent is the word "alleluia." It's not sung or said from the night before Ash Wednesday until it rings out with renewed splendor on Easter Eve. (Absence really can make the heart grow fonder.)

FROM ASH WEDNESDAY UNTIL THE THIRD SUNDAY

Early Lent

The first two weeks of Lent are devoted to beginning the "paschal season" — the span of days from Ash Wednesday until Pentecost.

The classroom might get cleaned and the decor simplified. A lenten corner can be set up to highlight symbols of the season, such as the tree of knowledge, Noah's ark or signs of the desert. Here you can share the ways students are keeping Lent this year.

A focus of the first weeks of Lent is on renewing our yearlong life of prayer, self-sacrifice and the sharing of charity. During Lent we explore ways to do these things well. The season is a rehearsal for a wholesome way of life.

Readings
The *Lectionary for Masses with Children* has nine sets of readings for lenten weekdays. The first set, #176, is probably best for Ash Wednesday and early Lent.

Set #176 has four options for a gospel reading, all four from Ash Wednesday's reading from Matthew about Jesus' advice on prayer, fasting and almsgiving. The first option is the full reading. The other options are shorter and emphasize either almsgiving, prayer or fasting.

Sets #178 and 179 include passages from Matthew that continue Jesus' teaching on prayer. These also are fine readings for the early weeks of Lent.

Psalm Refrain
Psalm 51, *"Be merciful, O Lord, for we have sinned."*
Or Psalm 91, *"Be with me, Lord, when I am in trouble."*

Hymns
"Again we keep this solemn fast" *(the text is a lenten "classic")*
"Amazing grace" *(this is wonderful as a round)*
"Lord, who throughout these forty days"
"Now we remain" *(a communion song for Lent)*
"O Sun of justice" *(another classic text, set to a chant melody)*
"Somebody's knockin' at your door" *(perfect for the sacrament of reconciliation)*
"Ubi caritas"

Sample Intercessions
For the church in these days of Lent . . .
For the people who are preparing to be baptized at Easter . . .
For everyone who struggles against evil . . .
For the courage to live a good life . . .
For all of us during this holy season . . .

FROM THE THIRD SUNDAY UNTIL THE FIFTH SUNDAY

MID-LENT

A very strong and ancient paschal tradition is to proclaim and to celebrate the scripture stories of our salvation — the stories of creation, of Adam and Eve, of Noah, of Sarah and Abraham, of Isaac and Rebekah and their children and grandchildren, of Miriam and Moses, of Judith and Esther and Jonah and Daniel, and even more.

All this storytelling takes time. Perhaps that's why we have 40 days to keep Lent and 50 to keep Easter. One old custom is to make a "burning bush." In the classroom, as the scripture stories are told, the characters and their symbols are fashioned out of paper and then hung on branches that have been arranged in a pot of sand. You also might include stories of the saints and of modern-day peacemakers and prophets.

A custom for the middle of Lent is for the church to honor someone who seems to live a life of prayer, fasting (simple living) and almsgiving (charity). Students can keep this custom. They would select someone from the news, from history or from the community to receive, either in person or in spirit, a "laetare rose." (This is named after Laetare — "rejoice" — Sunday, an old title for the Fourth Sunday of Lent.) The recipient's work would be researched and can be highlighted in a special display.

Readings
Among the nine sets of lenten weekday readings in the children's lectionary, sets #180 – 183 seem especially suited to the middle weeks of the season.

Set #180 includes part of the tale of Joseph and his brothers, a traditional lenten scripture. It would be worthwhile to tell the whole story in class in preparation for this reading.

The gospel paired with this story, Matthew 5:20 – 24, begins with harsh words spoken out of context: "Jesus said, 'You must obey God's commands better than the Pharisees . . . obey them.'" Perhaps this reading would be stronger if the first paragraph were skipped so that the reading began, "Jesus said to his disciples, 'You know that our ancestors were told . . .'"

Psalm Refrain
Psalm 51, *"Be merciful, O Lord, for we have sinned."*
Or Psalm 91, *"Be with me, Lord, when I am in trouble."*

Hymns
See the suggestions for Lent on page 71.

Intercessions
For forgiveness and charity . . .
For discipline and self-control . . .
For a wholesome way of life . . .
For the people who are going to be baptized this Easter . . .
For all of us gathered here . . .

FROM THE FIFTH SUNDAY UNTIL HOLY THURSDAY

LATE LENT

Some places hold a kind of pep rally to encourage student participation in the Triduum. No doubt there are songs to learn, scriptures to study and ceremonies to rehearse. In all of this, try to communicate some of the wonder and awe at the arrival of our most sacred, most beloved festival.

The Triduum begins Holy Thursday evening. Until then it is Lent. It's not appropriate to celebrate a Triduum liturgy, such as the Mass of the Lord's Supper, until the Triduum actually begins. Starting on page 90, the *Leader's Manual* of the *Hymnal for Catholic Students* offers fine suggestions for a service for Holy Thursday afternoon or morning (or even earlier in the week) that helps us say goodbye to Lent.

Among students, these are good days for spring cleaning and for helping out with the many parish preparations for the Triduum liturgies and for Palm Sunday, too. These activities, practical as they are, can be prayer-in-action.

For many children, a communal celebration of the sacrament of reconciliation marks the completion of Lent; see readings #488 – 491 for this sacrament.

Readings

Set #184 of the nine sets for lenten weekdays seems the most appropriate for the end of Lent. However, the gospel passage (John 11:47 – 52), about the Pharisees plotting to kill Jesus, may conflict with a principle used to select readings for this lectionary: "Also omitted were . . . readings children could perceive as anti-Semitic." (Introduction to the *Lectionary for Masses with Children,* 17)

Here's an alternative:

First reading #488-1 (from the readings for reconciliation):
Ephesians 5:1 – 2, 8 – 10, *"Christ offered his life for us."*
Gospel #370 (from the feast of the Holy Cross):
John 3:13 – 17, *"God loved the world so much . . ."*

Psalm Refrain

Psalm 51, *"Be merciful, O Lord, for we have sinned."*
Or Psalm 91, *"Be with me, Lord, when I am in trouble."*

Hymns

In the final days before the Triduum, songs of the passion and death of the Lord are added to the lenten songs (see page 71):
"Jesu, Jesu, fill us with your love"
"Jesus, remember me"
"Were you there"
"What wondrous love is this"

Sample Intercessions

For all people who are treated unfairly . . .
For the dying . . .
For prisoners in jail . . .
For all who soon will be baptized . . .
For a blessed Easter . . .

The Paschal Triduum

FROM HOLY THURSDAY EVENING UNTIL EASTER SUNDAY AFTERNOON

It's just about impossible to exaggerate the importance of the Triduum in the life of the church. All of us are asked to put everything else aside in order to keep these days free from work, from entertainment, even from the distraction of preparing meals. (That's one reason for the fasting of Good Friday and Holy Saturday, and why so many customary Easter foods, such as ham and eggs, are made ahead of time and then refrigerated.)

Well before the Triduum, schedules must be cleared to allow us all to celebrate these holiest of holy days.

The Triduum is the year's heart. We immerse ourselves in the core of the good news — the death, burial and resurrection of Jesus Christ. And it's not something "long ago and far away" that we celebrate. In baptism and the eucharist — the "Easter sacraments" — the Passover of Christ from death to life happens here and now, here among us.

Wonder upon wonder, during the Christian Passover the church also celebrates the creation of the world, the great flood, Abraham's near-sacrifice of Isaac, and the slaves' exodus from Egypt to the promised land.

And if that weren't enough, the Triduum is also the festival of Jonah's journey in the whale, of Esther freeing her people, of Daniel's stay with the lions, of the three children passing unharmed through the fiery furnace.

The *Lectionary for Masses with Children* does not have readings for the Triduum. The notion here is that everyone of every age hears the same readings from the regular lectionary.

Participation in the liturgies of the Triduum is not optional. It's essential. An ancient poet put it this way: All of us must be present for the paschal festival, for we are members of the body of Christ, and how can this body rise in glory if parts of it are missing?

School-age children really should be expected to participate in the Triduum. And, to the best of their abilities, they should be given a share in the preparations. Some fine suggestions for doing this can be found in LTP's *The Three Days,* by Gabe Huck.

In parishes that celebrate the liturgy with care, it's often the children who are most entranced by the ritual — by the foot washings, the veneration of the cross, the Easter bonfire, the storytelling, the baptisms, and by the extraordinary celebration of the eucharist.

That's where all of us belong and where all of us are welcome during the Christian Passover.

Eastertime

FROM EASTER SUNDAY UNTIL PENTECOST

Eastertime is 50 days long. Fifty days is "a week of weeks" plus a day, an emblem of eternity. Eastertime is for living with one foot in heaven.

In much of North America, this can be a heavenly time of year. It's spring! Apple trees bloom, birds return, days are long and getting longer. We open our windows, we play softball, we plant geraniums, and we may even think lazy thoughts.

Eastertime brings Earth Day and May Day and Mother's Day. It's the perfect season for baptisms, confirmations and first communions. There are hikes, picnics, bicycle trips, and more than the usual number of class outings to museums, theaters and amusement parks. No matter where we go, like the disciples on the road to Emmaus, we can expect to meet the risen Christ.

Especially when the Triduum falls in mid- or late April, the Easter season brings us near to the end of the school year, with its dances, honors ceremonies, graduation and farewells. These, too, are a part of Eastertime, a season acquainted with endings that lead to new beginnings.

During Eastertime, if you celebrate the eucharist on a saint's day, you can choose from the readings from the Proper of Saints, but it also would be appropriate to choose from the eight sets of weekday readings for the Easter season.

However, there are a few feast days when the readings should be chosen just from the Proper of Saints: Mark (April 25), Philip and James (May 3), Matthias (May 14) and the Visit of the Virgin Mary to Elizabeth (May 31).

In Eastertime the first reading usually is a passage from the Acts of the Apostles. This sequel to Luke's gospel is like a family album of the early church. Among its tales are ones about a riot, a shipwreck and a shifty deal. Some narratives are long, but don't avoid a reading just because it's long. Everyone enjoys a good story.

Sometimes Acts has harsh words: for instance, Peter's accusations against religious leaders (Acts 5:27 – 32, #189). Unless you are prepared to explain this harsh attitude to students, it might be best to avoid choosing this passage.

If the solemnity of the Ascension is a school day, you'll certainly want to fill it with festivities — a splendid liturgy and perhaps a dress-up day, a special lunch menu, an afternoon party, a chance to do some cloud-gazing in anticipation of the joys of heaven.

Readings for Ascension are in the Sunday volumes of the children's lectionary, which gives a special rule: At a parish Mass, these readings "may be used only when . . . the liturgy of the word for the children is held in a place apart from the main assembly." However, at a school Mass or a Mass specially scheduled for children, the readings from the children's lectionary may be used.

In church, be sure to light the paschal candle for every celebration from Easter Sunday until Pentecost. Some classes set up their own paschal candle for the season, put alongside or right inside a bowl of blessed water, where the candle can burn safely. The candle and the water are Eastertime reminders of baptism.

FROM EASTER MONDAY UNTIL THE FOURTH SUNDAY

EARLY EASTERTIME

Plan something festive, such as an egg hunt, for the first school days of Eastertime. It will communicate far more than words that Easter isn't over, that Easter is a 50-day season.

A weekday Easter Mass with children is perfectly appropriate any day in these first weeks of the season. It might include an entrance procession with someone carrying in the paschal candle and a generous sprinkling of baptismal water. (This is a Sunday ritual that might also be at home on weekdays during the Easter season.) Now also is a good time to make sure the bread and wine used for the eucharist with children is well made, perhaps even homemade.

In the classroom, don't be too quick to take down Easter decorations: for instance, eggs, lambs, rabbits, peacocks, butterflies. But you might make sure the designs aren't sappy. These symbols aren't only for very young children.

Flowers can be kept near the classroom cross, a tree of life. The prayer corner can feature a bowl of baptismal water, used to sign ourselves each morning. Some classes create a special display on the ways that students help bring the peace of the risen Christ to each other and to the community.

Readings

There are eight sets of readings for Eastertime weekdays.

The first set, #185, with its wonderful gospel about Mary Magdalene meeting the risen Jesus, is the best choice for Mass during the Easter octave, and it's probably the first choice if you are celebrating just one weekday Mass with the children during these early weeks of the Easter season.

Psalm Refrain

Psalm 114, *"God has freed us and redeemed us with his mighty arm."*

Or Psalm 118, *"This is the day the Lord has made."*

Hymns

"I am the bread of life"

"I received the living God" *(a fine communion song for the season)*

"Jesus Christ is risen today"

"Lift high the cross"

"O sons and daughters" *(a French Easter carol)*

"That Easter day with joy was bright" *(from a Latin carol)*

"You have put on Christ" *(this is a round to sing during a baptism; change the "you" to "we" to sing at other times)*

Sample Intercessions

That the peace of Christ will stop all fighting . . .

That we may learn to see Christ in every stranger . . .

That the earth will be made as clean
as the day it was created . . .

That spring will be free from bad storms . . .

That everything that has died will be raised to new life . . .

FROM THE FOURTH SUNDAY UNTIL THE DAY BEFORE THE ASCENSION

MID-EASTERTIME

In many places, these days coincide with the full flowering of spring. It's Maytime, the delightful month that always brings with it two important Easter images. One is the Good Shepherd, the risen Christ who gave his life for his sheep. The other is Jesus' mother Mary, who once stood by the foot of the cross and now reigns joyfully as the *Regina caeli,* the Queen of heaven.

Someone might search out the beautiful and simple chant *"Regina caeli"* and teach it. This chant is a Roman Catholic "golden oldie," one of our treasures. Even in Latin it's easy to learn. During Eastertime this chant replaces the *Angelus* prayer. Some people sing it every night during Eastertime just before going to bed.

During Eastertime keep some spring flowers by a statue or other image of Mary. In the children's lectionary, two fine Eastertime readings for a liturgy of the word for a May crowning ceremony are from the Common of the Blessed Virgin Mary: #448-1, Acts 1:12 – 13, 14, "After Jesus' ascension, Mary and the other disciples stayed together in prayer"; and #451-3, John 19:25 – 27, "Jesus' mother stood beside the cross."

Readings

Among the eight sets of readings for Eastertime weekdays, sets #187, 188, 190 and 192 seem well suited to these weeks.

If there's one Mass during this time, perhaps set #190 would be the first choice. These readings set before us the beloved image of the Good Shepherd as well as one of the accounts from the Acts of the Apostles of the conversion of Saul, who soon would call himself Paul.

Psalm Refrain

Psalm 23, *"My shepherd is the Lord."*
Or Psalm 118, *"This is the day the Lord has made."*

Hymns

Other suggestions for Eastertime hymns are on page 81.

"Alleluia, sing to Jesus" *(also a fine song for the Ascension)*
"I received the living God"
"The Lord, the Lord, the Lord is my shepherd" *(a lively spiritual)*

Sample Intercessions

For all the people who were baptized on Easter Eve . . .
For those who are confirmed this year . . .
For those who celebrate their first communion this year . . .
For everyone who tries to be a good shepherd . . .
For all of us gathered here . . .

FROM ASCENSION UNTIL PENTECOST
LATE EASTERTIME

Ascension Day is not Jesus' farewell, which would make it a sad occasion. It's an Eastertime celebration of Jesus' glorious presence. Where Christ has gone we are called to follow.

A nice custom for the day is for students to surround the shining paschal candle with a "cloud" of some kind; crabapple blossoms would be beautiful; add to that some fragrant incense. It's a good day for brass instruments and for singing Psalm 47, "God mounts his throne to shouts of joy: a blare of trumpets for the Lord!"

The nine-day period after Ascension is the Pentecost novena. (Novena is Latin for "nine.") Any novena of prayer is patterned after these nine days, when the disciples gathered in the upper room to wait for Jesus to send the Holy Spirit.

Just like all the big days of the church, Pentecost has its songs and foods (cheesecake is one) and decorations (for instance, newly green tree branches). These things are important because we just don't think about festivals — we taste and smell and see them, and we even sing and dance for them, too.

Of course, Pentecost falls on a Sunday, but it would be wonderful in the classroom to prepare for Pentecost throughout the novena.

Readings

Among the eight sets of readings for Eastertime weekdays, sets #189 and 191 seem especially suited to the days between the Ascension and Pentecost.

Perhaps a first reading can be selected from #479, from the readings for Confirmation; for instance, Joel 3:1 – 3 (#479-2) seems perfect for the Pentecost novena; it is part of one of the church's readings for Pentecost Eve.

Psalm Refrain

Psalm 47, *"God mounts his throne to shouts of joy"* (especially for Ascension Day).
Or Psalm 104, *"Lord, send out your Spirit"* (especially for the Pentecost novena).

Hymns

"Lord, you give the great commission" *(good from now until the end of the school year)*
"O breathe on me, O Breath of God" *(set to a gentle Irish tune that can be sung as a round)*
"O Holy Spirit, by whose breath" *(set to the classic chant* Veni, Creator Spiritus)
"Send us your Spirit"
"Veni, Sancte Spiritus"

Sample Intercessions

For the coming of the Holy Spirit . . .
For the Spirit's help in everything we do . . .
For good weather for planting the crops . . .
For our friendships to grow strong . . .
For a successful finish to the year . . .

Summer Ordinary Time

Begins the Day After Pentecost

It can be hard to get a handle on Ordinary Time. That's because it's not a season the way Lent and Eastertime are. Notice that the children's lectionary says "Season of Advent" and "Season of Easter," but Ordinary Time is just called "Ordinary Time." It's what we call the weeks in between the seasons.

During Ordinary Time we might concern ourselves with the Lord's Day, the weekly festival of Christians. How well is it kept? How can we prepare for it during the week? We probably have some work to do in fostering the celebration of Sunday.

Summer is blest with festival days. The Birth of John the Baptist, June 24, is a wonderful one to keep with children. It's the Midsummer Nativity! In some places it's kept with the same gusto as Christmas. This is a fine occasion to kick off parish and school summertime activities and programs.

A few days later, June 29, is the solemnity of Saints Peter and Paul, the "founding fathers" of the church. Then there's Canada Day and Independence Day. Summer makes a grand entrance. A custom that these days have in common is that they all have been celebrated with bonfires and fireworks, which is only natural so soon after the summer solstice.

The sun is an emblem of the summer festivals. When John was born, his father sang that the sun will shine on those trapped in darkness. On Transfiguration Day, August 6, we hear that Jesus himself became as bright as the sun. On Assumption Day, August 15, we hear from Revelation about a woman clothed with the sun.

On these two August days, we bless God for the seas, for the skies, for garden produce, for all this material world that one day will be transfigured, with Jesus and Mary, into glory. These days might mark the end of parish and school summer programs.

Liturgical celebrations with children don't always have to be Mass. Often Morning Prayer or Evening Prayer would be perfect. These are "official" liturgies of the church, and they usually include an opening song, one or more psalms, a brief reading, intercessions and the Our Father. The *Lectionary for Masses with Children* can be a source for the reading.

With its thanksgiving for light, it's hard to imagine a more wonderful setting for Evening Prayer than around a campfire or barbecue grill. And Morning Prayer, with its remembrance of baptism, might be perfect by a poolside, a fountain or near any body of water.

FROM PENTECOST UNTIL THE END OF THE SCHOOL YEAR
ORDINARY TIME

When the weather grows warm we all get antsy to be outdoors. Summer vacation can't arrive soon enough. Still, there can be trepidation as school ends — about farewells, about a coming summer job, about what to do with time on our hands.

Some religious education programs and schools begin the year with a "Mass of the Holy Spirit." It may even be better to end the year, so soon after Pentecost, with prayer for the guidance and power of the Spirit.

Of course you want to celebrate the graduates! But keep in mind that all of us are "graduating" a bit at the end of each school year. You surely will want to have an opportunity for the students to say farewell to the graduates. There may be other farewells — to staff members not returning, to students moving to a new school.

This can be too busy a time for reviewing the past year, but it might be the only time to assess the liturgical life of students. One worthwhile question is whether or not we built up *repertory* — of psalms, songs, rituals and gestures. Did we repeat these things enough to have them sink into our hearts and minds? Will we return to them next year so they can stir memories and offer a sense of continuity?

Readings
The *Lectionary for Masses with Children* has readings "for the end of the school year." First reading #497 (Colossians 3:12, 15 – 17, "Be gentle, kind, humble, meek, patient") and gospel #500-1 (Matthew 13:31 – 32, the parable of the mustard seed) seem very fine for an end-of-the-school-year liturgy.
Or #223:

Galatians 5:22 – 23, 25 – 26, *"God's Spirit makes us loving, kind and gentle."*

John 14:15 – 17, *"The Spirit will show you what is true."*

Or #224 (which is also suitable to times of war or other troubles):

Isaiah 11:1, 5 – 9, *"Wolves and lambs will lie down together."*

John 14:27, *"I give you peace, so don't be afraid."*

Psalm Refrain
Psalm 96, *"Great is the Lord, worthy of praise."*
Or Psalm 34, *"Taste and see the goodness of the Lord."*

Hymns
"Jesu, Jesu, fill us with your love"
"Lord, you give the great commission"
"Now thank we all our God"

Some places have an end-of-the-year sing-along: They repeat psalms and songs they used the past year — a great idea! That becomes a way to end the old year and to look forward to a new year.

Sample Intercessions
For the people of the parish . . .
For teachers and students . . .
For blessings at the end of the year . . .
For children everywhere . . .
For a healthy, happy summer . . .

SUMMER VACATION
ORDINARY TIME

It might be vacation time, but it's also summer school time, camp time, Bible school time, picnic and barbecue time. These are days for any number of warm weather activities with children.

In summer we celebrate the Birth of John (June 24), Saints Peter and Paul (June 29), the Transfiguration of the Lord (August 6) and the Assumption of Mary (August 15). We remember several beloved saints — Thomas, Maria Goretti, Benedict, Kateri, Mary Magdalene, Bridget, James, Anne and Joachim, Martha, Dominic, Lawrence, Clare, Bartholomew, and many more.

When preparing Mass, remember that on days ranked as "solemnities" or "feasts" the readings must be chosen from the ones special for the day; these are found in the section of the lectionary called the "Proper of Saints."

There are 39 sets of readings for weekdays in Ordinary Time. On days that aren't solemnities or feasts, you can choose from the first 35 sets or from the "Masses for Various Needs and Occasions," and on a saint's day you also can choose from appropriate readings in the Proper of Saints.

Readings
Of the sets of readings for Ordinary Time, you might try to match something in the readings to the circumstances of the eucharist. For instance, Mass at summer camp might include the gospel account of Jesus calming the sea, #204, Mark 4:35 – 41.

A liturgy especially prepared for small children might include readings about children, for example, #206:
1 John 2:29 — 3:1, *"The Father lets us be called his children."*
Mark 9:33 – 37, *"When you welcome a child because of me, you welcome me."*

Psalm Refrain
Psalm 23, *"My shepherd is the Lord."*
Or Psalm 27, *"The Lord is my light and my salvation."*

Hymns
"All things bright and beautiful"
"Let all things now living"
"Lord of all hopefulness"
"Seek ye first the kingdom of God"
"Shalom chaverim"
"Shout for joy, loud and long"

Most any of the songs suggested for autumn also seem suited to summer.

Sample Intercessions
For the church throughout the world . . .
For the nations and peoples of the earth . . .
For those in any kind of trouble . . .
For those who have died . . .
For everyone here . . .

DIRECTORY FOR

MASSES WITH CHILDREN

OUTLINE

INTRODUCTION

1. The Church must show special concern for baptized children who have yet to be fully initiated through the sacraments of confirmation and eucharist as well as for children who have only recently been admitted to holy communion. Today the circumstances in which children grow up are not favorable to their spiritual progress.[1] In addition parents sometimes scarcely fulfill the obligations they accepted at the baptism of their children to bring them up as Christians.

2. In the upbringing of children in the Church a special difficulty arises from the fact that liturgical celebrations, especially the eucharist, cannot fully exercise their inherent pedagogical force upon children.[2] Although the vernacular may now be used at Mass, still the words and signs have not been sufficiently adapted to the capacity of children.

In fact, even in daily life children do not always understand all their experiences with adults but rather may find them boring. It cannot therefore be expected of the liturgy that everything must always be intelligible to them. Nonetheless, we may fear spiritual harm if over the years children repeatedly experience in the Church things that are barely comprehensible: recent psychological study has established how profoundly children are formed by the religious experience of infancy and early childhood, because of the special religious receptivity proper to those years.[3]

3. The Church follows its Master, who "put his arms around the children and blessed them" (Mk 10:16). It cannot leave children in the condition described. Vatican Council II had spoken in the Constitution on the Liturgy about the need of liturgical adaptation for various groups.[4] Soon afterwards, especially in the first Synod of Bishops held in Rome in 1967, the Church began to consider how participation by children could be easier. On the occasion of the Synod, the President of the Consilium for the Implementation of the Constitution on the Liturgy said explicitly that it could not be a matter of "creating some entirely special rite but rather of retaining, shortening, or omitting some elements or of making a better selection of texts."[5]

4. All the details of eucharistic celebration with a congregation were determined in the General Instruction of the revised Roman Missal published in 1969. Then this Congregation began to prepare a special Directory for Masses with Children, as a supplement to the General Instruction. This was done in response to repeated petitions from the entire Catholic world and with the cooperation of men and women specialists from almost every nation.

5. Like the *General Instruction of the Roman Missal*, this Directory reserves some adaptations to the conference of bishops or to individual bishops.[6]

Some adaptations of the Mass may be necessary for children in a given country but cannot be included in a general directory. In accord with the *Constitution on the Liturgy* art. 40, the conferences of bishops are to propose such adaptations to the Apostolic See for introduction into the liturgy with its consent.

6. The Directory is concerned with children who have not yet entered the period of preadolescence. It does not speak directly of children who are physically or mentally handicapped, because a broader adaptation is sometimes necessary for them.[7] Nevertheless, the following norms may also be applied to the handicapped, with the necessary changes.

7. The first chapter of the Directory (nos. 8 – 15) gives a kind of foundation by considering the different ways in which children are introduced to the eucharistic liturgy. The second chapter briefly treats Masses with adults in which children also take part (nos. 16 – 19). Finally, the third chapter (nos. 20 – 54) treats at greater length Masses with children in which only some adults take part.

Chapter I
The Introduction of Children to the Eucharistic Celebration

8. A fully Christian life is inconceivable without participation in the liturgical services in which the faithful, gathered into a single assembly, celebrate the paschal mystery. Therefore, the religious initiation of children must be in harmony with this purpose.[8] The Church baptizes children and therefore, relying on the gifts conferred by this sacrament, it must be concerned that once baptized they grow in communion with Christ and each other. The sign and pledge of that communion is participation in the eucharistic table, for which children are being prepared or led to a deeper realization of its meaning. This liturgical and eucharistic formation may not be separated from their general education, both human and Christian; indeed it would be harmful if their liturgical formation lacked such a basis.

9. For this reason all who have a part in the formation of children should consult and work together toward one objective: that even if children already have some feeling for God and the things of God, they may also experience in proportion to their age and personal development the human values that are present in the eucharistic celebration. These values include the community activity, exchange of greetings, capacity to listen and to seek and grant pardon, expression of gratitude, experience of symbolic actions, a meal of friendship, and festive celebration.[9]

Eucharistic catechesis, dealt with in no. 12, should develop such human values. Then, depending on their age and their psychological and social situation, children will gradually open their minds to the perception of Christian values and the celebration of the mystery of Christ.[10]

10. The Christian family has the greatest role in instilling these Christian and human values.[11] Thus Christian education, provided by parents and other educators, should be strongly encouraged in relation to the liturgical formation of children as well.

By reason of the duty in conscience freely accepted at the baptism of their children, parents are bound to teach them gradually how to pray. This they do by praying with them each day and by introducing them to prayers said privately.[12] If children, prepared in this way even from their early years, take part in the Mass with their family when they wish, they will easily begin to sing and to pray in the liturgical community and indeed will already have some initial idea of the eucharistic mystery.

If the parents are weak in faith but still wish their children to receive Christian formation, they should be urged at least to communicate to their children the human values mentioned already and, when the occasion arises, to participate in meetings of parents and in noneucharistic celebrations held with children.

11. The Christian communities to which the individual families belong or in which the children live also have a responsibility toward children baptized in the Church. By giving witness to the Gospel, living communal charity, and actively celebrating the mysteries of Christ, the Christian community is an excellent school of Christian and liturgical formation for the children who live in it.

Within the Christian community, godparents or other persons noted for their dedicated service can, out of apostolic zeal, contribute greatly to the necessary catechesis in the case of families that fail in their obligation toward the children's Christian upbringing.

Preschool programs, Catholic schools, and various kinds of associations for children serve these same ends in a special way.

12. Even in the case of children, the liturgy itself always exerts its own inherent power to instruct.[13] Yet within religious education programs in the schools and parishes the necessary importance should be given to catechesis on the Mass.[14] This catechesis should be directed to the child's active, conscious, and authentic participation.[15] "Suited to children's age and capabilities, it should, by means of the main rites and prayers of the Mass, aim at conveying its meaning, including what relates to taking part in the Church's life."[16] This is especially true of the text of the eucharistic prayer and of the acclamations by which the children take part in this prayer.

The catechesis preparing children for first communion calls for special mention. In it they should learn not only the truths of faith regarding the eucharist but also how from first communion on — after being prepared according to their capacity by penance — they can as full members of Christ's Body take part actively with the people of God in the eucharist, sharing in the Lord's table and the community of their brothers and sisters.

13. Various kinds of celebrations may also play a major role in the liturgical formation of children and in their preparation for the Church's liturgical life. By the very fact of such celebrations children easily come to appreciate some liturgical elements, for example, greetings, silence, and common praise (especially when this is sung together). But care must by taken that the instructive element does not become dominant in these celebrations.

14. Depending on the capacity of the children, the word of God should have a greater and greater place in these celebrations. In fact, as the children's spiritual capacity develops, celebrations of the word of God in the strict sense should be held frequently, especially during Advent and Lent.[17] These will help greatly to develop in the children an appreciation of the word of God.

15. While all that has been said remains true, the final purpose of all liturgical and eucharistic formation must be a greater and greater conformity to the Gospel in the daily life of the children.

Chapter II
Masses with Adults in Which Children also Participate

16. In many places parish Masses are celebrated, especially on Sundays and holy days, at which a good many children take part along with the large number of adults. On such occasions the witness of adult believers can have a great effect upon the children. Adults can in turn benefit spiritually from experiencing the part that the children have within the Christian community. The Christian spirit of the family is greatly fostered when children take part in these Masses together with their parents and other family members.

Infants who as yet are unable or unwilling to take part in the Mass may be brought in at the end of Mass to be blessed together with the rest of the community. This may be done, for example, if parish helpers have been taking care of them in a separate area.

17. Nevertheless, in Masses of this kind it is necessary to take great care that the children present do not feel neglected because of their inability to participate or to understand what happens and what is proclaimed in the celebration. Some account should be taken of their presence: for example, by speaking to them directly in the introductory comments (as at the beginning and the end of Mass) and at some point in the homily.

Sometimes, moreover, if the place itself and the nature of the community permit, it will be appropriate to celebrate the liturgy of the word, including a homily, with the children in a separate, but not too distant, room. Then, before the eucharistic liturgy begins, the children are led to the place where the adults have meanwhile celebrated their own liturgy of the word.

18. It may also be very helpful to give some tasks to the children. They may, for example, bring forward the gifts or perform one or other of the songs of the Mass.

19. If the number of children is large, it may at times be suitable to plan the Mass so that it corresponds more closely to the needs of the children. In this case the homily should be directed to them but in such a way that adults may also benefit from it. Wherever the bishop permits, in addition to the adaptations already provided in the Order of Mass, one or other of the particular adaptations described later in the Directory may be employed in a Mass celebrated with adults in which children also participate.

CHAPTER III
MASSES WITH CHILDREN IN WHICH ONLY A FEW ADULTS PARTICIPATE

20. In addition to the Masses in which children take part with their parents and other family members (which are not always possible everywhere), Masses with children in which only a few adults take part are recommended, especially during the week. From the beginning of the liturgical reform it has been clear to everyone that some adaptations are necessary in these Masses.

Such adaptations, but only those of a more general kind, will be considered later (nos. 38 – 54).

21. It is always necessary to keep in mind that these eucharistic celebrations must lead children toward the celebration of Mass with adults, especially the Masses at which the Christian community must come together on Sundays.[19] Thus, apart from adaptations that are necessary because of the children's age, the result should not be entirely special rites, markedly different from the Order of Mass celebrated with a congregation.[20] The purpose of the various elements should always correspond with what is said in the *General Instruction of the Roman Missal* on individual points, even if at times for pastoral reasons an absolute *identity* cannot be insisted upon.

OFFICES AND MINISTRIES IN THE CELEBRATION

22. The principles of active and conscious participation are in a sense even more significant for Masses celebrated with children. Every effort should therefore be made to increase this participation and to make it more intense. For this reason as many children as possible should have special parts in the celebration: for example, preparing the place and the altar (see no. 29), acting as cantor (see no. 24), singing in a choir, playing musical instruments (see no. 32), proclaiming the readings (see nos. 24 and 47), responding during the homily (see no. 48), reciting the intentions of the general intercessions, bringing the gifts to the altar, and performing similar activities in accord with the usage of various peoples (see no. 34).

To encourage participation, it will sometimes be helpful to have several additions, for example, the insertion of motives for giving thanks before the priest begins the dialogue of the preface.

In all this, it should be kept in mind that external activities will be fruitless and even harmful if they do not serve the internal participation of the children. Thus religious silence has its importance even in Masses with children (see no. 37). The children should not be allowed to forget that all the forms of participation reach their high point in eucharistic communion, when the body and blood of Christ are received as spiritual nourishment.[21]

23. It is the responsibility of the priest who celebrates with children to make the celebration festive, familial, and meditative.[22] Even more than in Masses with adults, the priest is the one to create this kind of attitude, which depends on his personal preparation and his manner of acting and speaking with others.

The priest should be concerned above all about the dignity, clarity, and simplicity of his actions and gestures. In speaking to the children he should express himself so that he will be easily understood, while avoiding any childish style of speech.

The free use of introductory comments[23] will lead children to a genuine liturgical participation, but these should be more than mere explanatory remarks.

It will help him to reach the hearts of the children if the priest sometimes expresses the invitations in his own words, for example, at the penitential rite, the prayer over the gifts, the Lord's Prayer, the sign of peace, and communion.

24. Since the eucharist is always the action of the entire ecclesial community, the participation of at least some adults is desirable. These should be present not as monitors but as participants, praying with the children and helping them to the extent necessary.

With the consent of the pastor or rector of the church, one of the adults may speak to the children after the gospel, especially if the priest finds it difficult to adapt himself to the mentality of children. In this matter the norms soon to be issued by the Congregation for the Clergy should be observed.

Even in Masses with children attention is to be paid to the diversity of ministries so that the Mass may stand out clearly as the celebration of a community.[24] For example, readers and cantors, whether children or adults, should be employed. In this way a variety of voices will keep the children from becoming bored.

PLACE AND TIME OF CELEBRATION

25. The primary place for the eucharistic celebration for children is the church. Within the church, however, a space should be carefully chosen, if available, that will be suited to the number of participants. It should be a place where the children can act with a feeling of ease according to the requirements of a living liturgy that is suited to their age.

If the church does not satisfy these demands, it will sometimes be suitable to celebrate the eucharist with children outside a place of worship. But in that case the place chosen should be appropriate and worthy of the celebration.[25]

26. The time of day chosen for Masses with children should correspond to the circumstances of their lives so that they may be most open to hearing the word of God and to celebrating the eucharist.

27. Weekday Mass in which children participate can certainly be celebrated with greater effect and less danger of boredom if it does not take place every day (for example, in boarding schools). Moreover, preparation can be more careful if there is a longer interval between diverse celebrations.

Sometimes it will be preferable to have common prayer, to which the children may contribute spontaneously, or else a common meditation, or a celebration of the word of God. These are ways of continuing the eucharistic celebrations already held and of leading to a deeper participation in subsequent celebrations.

28. When the number of children who celebrate the eucharist together is very great, attentive and conscious participation becomes more difficult. Therefore, if possible, several groups should be formed; these should not be set up rigidly according to age but with regard for the children's progress in religious formation and catechetical preparation.

During the week such groups may be invited to the sacrifice of the Mass on different days.

PREPARATION FOR THE CELEBRATION

29. Each eucharistic celebration with children should be carefully prepared beforehand, especially with regard to the prayers, songs, readings, and intentions of the general intercessions. This should be done in discussion with the adults and with the children who will have a special ministry in these Masses. If possible, some of the children should take part in preparing and ornamenting the place of celebration and preparing the chalice with the paten and the cruets. Presupposing the appropriate internal participation, such activity will help to develop the spirit of community celebration.

SINGING AND MUSIC

30. Singing must be given great importance in all celebrations, but it is to be especially encouraged in every way for Masses celebrated with children, in view of their special affinity for music.[26] The culture of various peoples and the capabilities of the children present should be taken into account.

If possible, the acclamations should be sung by the children rather than recited, especially the acclamations that form part of the eucharistic prayer.

31. To facilitate the children's participation in singing the *Gloria, Credo, Sanctus,* and *Agnus Dei,* it is permissible to use with the melodies appropriate vernacular texts, accepted by competent authority, even if these do not correspond exactly to the liturgical texts.[27]

32. The use of "musical instruments can add a great deal" in Masses with children, especially if they are played by the children themselves.[28] The playing of instruments will help to sustain the singing or to encourage the reflection of the children; sometimes in their own fashion instruments express festive joy and the praise of God.

Care should always be taken, however, that the musical accompaniment does not overpower the singing or become a distraction rather than a help to the children. Music should correspond to the purpose intended for the different periods at which it is played during the Mass.

With these precautions and with due and special discretion, recorded music may also be used in Masses with children, in accord with norms established by the conferences of bishops.

GESTURES

33. In view of the nature of the liturgy as an activity of the entire person and in view of the psychology of children, participation by means of gestures and posture should be strongly encouraged in Masses with children, with due regard for age and local customs. Much depends not only on the actions of the priest,[29] but also on the manner in which the children conduct themselves as a community.

If, in accord with the norms of the *General Instruction of the Roman Missal,*[30] a conference of bishops adapts the congregation's actions at Mass to the mentality of a people, it should take the special condition of children into account or should decide on adaptations that are for children only.

34. Among the actions that are considered under this heading, processions and other activities that involve physical participation deserve special mention.

The children's entering in procession with the priest can serve to help them to experience a sense of the communion that is thus being created.[31] The participation of at least some children in the procession with the Book of the Gospels makes clear the presence of Christ announcing the word to his people. The procession of children with the chalice and the gifts expresses more clearly the value and meaning of the preparation of the gifts. The communion procession, if properly arranged, helps greatly to develop the children's devotion.

VISUAL ELEMENTS

35. The liturgy of the Mass contains many visual elements and these should be given great prominence with children. This is especially true of the particular visual elements in the course of the liturgical year, for example, the veneration of the cross, the Easter candle, the lights on the feast of the Presentation of the Lord, and the variety of colors and liturgical appointments.

In addition to the visual elements that belong to the celebration and to the place of celebration, it is appropriate to introduce other elements that will permit children to perceive visually the wonderful works of God in creation and redemption and thus support their prayer. The liturgy should never appear as something dry and merely intellectual.

36. For the same reason, the use of art work prepared by the children themselves may be useful, for example, as illustrations of a homily, as visual expressions of the intentions of the general intercessions, or as inspirations to reflection.

SILENCE

37. Even in Masses with children "silence should be observed at the designated times as part of the celebration"[32] lest too great a place be given to external action. In their own way children are genuinely capable of reflection. They need some guidance, however, so that they will learn how, in keeping with the different moments of the Mass (for example, after the homily or after communion[33]), to recollect themselves, meditate briefly, or praise God and pray to him in their hearts.[34]

Besides this, with even greater care than in Masses with adults, the liturgical texts should be proclaimed intelligibly and unhurriedly, with the necessary pauses.

PARTS OF THE MASS

38. The general structure of the Mass, which "is made up as it were of the liturgy of the word and the liturgy of the eucharist," should always be maintained, as should certain rites to open and conclude the celebration.[35] Within individual parts of the celebration, the adaptations that follow seem necessary if children are truly to experience, in their own way and according to the psychological patterns of childhood, "the mystery of faith ... by means of rites and prayers."[36]

39. Some rites and texts should never be adapted for children lest the difference between Masses with children and the Masses with adults become too pronounced.[37] These are "the acclamations and the responses to the priest's greeting,"[38] the Lord's Prayer, and the Trinitarian formulary at the end of the blessing with which the priest concludes the Mass. It is urged, moreover, that children should become accustomed to the Nicene Creed little by little, the right to use the Apostles' Creed indicated in no. 49 remaining intact.

A. Introductory Rite

40. The introductory rite of Mass has as its purpose "that the faithful coming together take on the form of a community and prepare themselves to listen to God's word and celebrate the eucharist properly."[39] Therefore every effort should be made to create this disposition in the children and not to jeopardize it by any excess of rites in this part of Mass.

It is sometimes proper to omit one or other element of the introductory rite or perhaps to expand one of the elements. There should always be at least some introductory element, which is completed by the opening prayer. In choosing individual elements, care should be taken that each one be used from time to time and that none be entirely neglected.

B. Reading and Explanation of the Word of God

41. Since readings taken from holy Scripture "form the main part of the liturgy of the word,"[40] even in Masses celebrated with children biblical reading should never be omitted.

42. With regard to the number of readings on Sundays and holy days, the decrees of the conferences of bishops are to be observed. If three or even two readings appointed on Sundays or weekdays can be understood by children only with difficulty, it is permissible to read two or only one of them, but the reading of the gospel should never be omitted.

43. If all the readings assigned to the day seem to be unsuited to the capacity of the children, it is permissible to choose readings or a reading either from the Lectionary of the Roman Missal or directly from the Bible, but taking into account the liturgical seasons. It is recommended, moreover, that the individual conferences of bishops see to the composition of lectionaries for Masses with children.

If, because of the limited capabilities of the children, it seems necessary to omit one or other verse of a biblical reading, this should be done cautiously and in such a way "that the meaning of the text or the intent and, as it were, style of the Scriptures are not distorted."[41]

44. In the choice of readings the criterion to be followed is the quality rather than the quantity of the texts from the Scriptures. A shorter reading is not as such always more suited to children than a lengthy reading. Everything depends on the spiritual advantage that the reading can bring to the children.

45. In the biblical texts "God is speaking to his people . . . and Christ is present to the faithful through his own word."[42] Paraphrases of Scripture should therefore be avoided. On the other hand, the use of translations that may already exist for the catechesis of children and that are accepted by the competent authority is recommended.

46. Verses of psalms, carefully selected in accord with the understanding of children, or singing in the form of psalmody or the *Alleluia* with a simple verse should be sung between the readings. The children should always have a part in this singing, but sometimes a reflective silence may be substituted for the singing.

If only a single reading is chosen, the singing may follow the homily.

47. All the elements that will help explain the readings should be given great consideration so that the children may make the biblical readings their own and may come more and more to appreciate the value of God's word.

Among such elements are the introductory comments that may precede the readings[43] and that by explaining the context or by introducing the text itself help the children to listen better and more fruitfully. The interpretation and explanation of the readings from the Scriptures in the Mass on a saint's day may include an account of the saint's life, not only in the homily but even before the readings in the form of an introduction.

When the text of the readings lends itself to this, it may be helpful to have the children read it with parts distributed among them, as is provided for the reading of the Lord's passion during Holy Week.

48. The homily explaining the word of God should be given great prominence in all Masses with children. Sometimes the homily intended for children should become a dialogue with them, unless it is preferred that they should listen in silence.

49. If the profession of faith occurs at the end of the liturgy of the word, the Apostle's Creed may be used with children, especially because it is part of their catechetical formation.

C. Presidential Prayers
50. The priest is permitted to choose from the Roman Missal texts of presidential prayers more suited to children, so that he may truly associate the children with himself. But he is to take into account the liturgical season.

51. Since these prayers were composed for adult Christians, however, the principle simply of choosing from among them does not serve the purpose of having the children regard the prayers as an expression of their own life and religious experience.[44] If this is the case, the text of prayers of the Roman Missal may be adapted to the needs of children, but this should be done in such a way that, preserving the purpose of the prayer and to some extent its substance as well, the priest avoids anything that is foreign to the literary genre of a presidential prayer, such as moral exhortations or a childish manner of speech.

52. The eucharistic prayer is of the greatest importance in the eucharist celebrated with children because it is the high point of the entire celebration.[45] Much depends on the manner in which the priest proclaims this prayer[46] and on the way the children take part by listening and making their acclamations.

The disposition of mind required for this central part of the celebration and the calm and reverence with which everything is done must make the children as attentive as possible. Their attention should be on the real presence of Christ on the altar under the elements of bread and wine, on his offering, on the thanksgiving through him and with him and in him, and on the Church's offering, which is made during the prayer and by which the faithful offer themselves and their lives with Christ to the eternal Father in the Holy Spirit.

For the present, the four eucharistic prayers approved by the supreme authority for Masses with adults and introduced into liturgical use are to be employed until the Apostolic See makes other provision for Masses with children.

D. Rites before Communion
53. When the eucharistic prayer has ended, the Lord's Prayer, the breaking of bread, and the invitation to communion should always follow,[47] that is, the elements that have the principal significance in the structure of this part of the Mass.

E. Communion and the Following Rites
54. Everything should be done so that the children who are properly disposed and who have already been admitted to the eucharist may go to the holy table calmly and with recollection and thus take part fully in the eucharistic mystery. If possible, there should be singing, suited to the children, during the communion procession.[48]

The comments that precede the final blessing[49] are important in Masses with children. Before they are dismissed they need some repetition and application of what they have heard, but this should be done in a very few words. In particular, this is the appropriate time to express the connection between the liturgy and life.

At least sometimes, depending on the liturgical seasons and different occasions in the children's life, the priest should use more expanded forms of blessing, but at the end should always retain the Trinitarian formulary with the sign of the cross.[50]

* * * * *

55. The contents of the Directory have as their purpose to help children readily and joyfully to encounter Christ together in the eucharistic celebration and to stand with him in the presence of the Father.[51] If they are formed by conscious and active participation in the eucharistic sacrifice and meal, they should learn day by day, at home and away from home, to proclaim Christ to others among their family and among their peers, by living the "faith, that works through love" (Gal 5:6).

This Directory was prepared by the Congregation for Divine Worship. On 22 October 1973, Pope Paul VI approved and confirmed it and ordered that it be published.

NOTES

1. See General Catechetical Directory [GCD] 5.
2. See Constitution on the Sacred Liturgy [CSL] 33.
3. See GCD 78.
4. See CSL 38; also *Actio pastoralis* [AP].
5. First Synod of Bishops, Liturgy: *Notitiae* 3 (1967) 368.
6. See Directory for Masses with Children [DMC] 19, 32, 33.
7. See Order of Mass with deaf and mute children of German-speaking regions approved, that is, confirmed by the Congregation for Divine Worship [CDW], 26 June 1970 (Prot. no. 1546/70).
8. See CSL 14, 19.
9. See GCD 25.
10. See Vatican Council II, Declaration on Christian Education, *Gravissimum educationis,* no. 2.
11. See ibid, 3.
12. See GCD 78.
13. See CSL 33.
14. See *Eucharisticum mysterium* [EM] 14.
15. See GCD 25.
16. See EM 14; GCD 57.
17. See CSL 35, 4.
18. See DMC 3.
19. See CSL 42, 106.
20. See First Synod of Bishops, Liturgy: *Notitiae* (1967) 368.
21. See General Instruction of the Roman Missal [GI] 56.
22. See DMC 37.
23. See GI 11.
24. See CSL 28.
25. See GI 253.
26. See GI 19.
27. See *Musicam sacram* [MS] 55.
28. MS 62.
29. See DMC 23.
30. See GI 21.
31. See GI 24.
32. GI 23.
33. See EM 38.
34. See GI 23.
35. GI 8.
36. CSL 48.
37. See DMC 21.
38. GI 15.
39. GI 24.
40. GI 33.
41. Lectionary for Mass: Introduction, 1969 edition, no. 7d.
42. GI 33.
43. See GI 11.
44. See Consilium for the Implementation of the Constitution on the Sacred Liturgy, instruction on translations of liturgical texts for celebrations with a congregation, 25 Jan 1969, no. 20: *Notitiae* 5 (1969) 7.
45. GI 54.
46. See DMC 23, 37.
47. See DMC 23.
48. See MS 32.
49. See GI 11.
50. See DMC 39.
51. See the Roman Missal [RM], Eucharistic Prayer II.

INTRODUCTION TO THE LECTIONARY FOR MASSES WITH CHILDREN

I. THE LITURGICAL CELEBRATION OF THE WORD OF GOD

Living Word of God

1. God speaks to us the Word, who has become flesh in Jesus Christ our Lord. Through him all things came to be and were made.[1] The many words spoken throughout history for our salvation have their origin and end in Christ Jesus.[2] In the liturgy we are called together that in the Spirit we may listen to and respond to the word of God in Christ. "That word constantly proclaimed in the liturgy is always, then, a living, active word through the power of the Holy Spirit. It expresses the Father's love that never fails in its effectiveness toward us."[3]

Word of God in the Assembly

2. The liturgical assembly is a gathering of God's holy People. Christ is present in the very act of gathering.[4] Christ is also present in the proclamation of the word of God.[5] This proclamation, if it is to promote a deeper experience of Christ's presence, must be understood in its most complete sense. It must be prepared for and experienced as the specific kind of event it is, namely, a ritual celebration composed of reading, dialogue in song, silence, and reflection, with the use of appropriate gestures and symbols. The ability to give assent to God's Good News is deeply influenced by the manner in which the word is proclaimed and celebrated in the liturgical assembly.[6] The Church's deepest calling is to praise God. Members of the Church do this by conforming their lives to the message of the Scriptures that they have heard and by bringing to the celebration of the liturgy all that they have done.[7]

God's Word in Story

3. Christian communities discover, express, and deepen their identity by sharing the stories of our salvation that we read in the Scriptures. The way we pass these biblical stories on to children will also influence the way in which the message of the Scriptures is communicated to the children.

Liturgy of the Word

4. One of the clearest aims and achievements of the liturgical reform after the Second Vatican Council has been the renewal of the scriptural elements of liturgical prayer and the wider opening of the Scriptures within the full cycle of liturgical seasons and celebrations.[8] Every sacramental rite, blessing, and hour of prayer calls for the proclamation of the word of God in the form of a liturgy of the word. The most effective realization of this proclamation is the eucharist, the visible word or sacrament of the paschal mystery into which we have been baptized. Full nourishment comes from the tables of God's word and eucharist.[9]

Liturgical Ministries

5. In its liturgy the Christian community acts in its capacity as an "ordered diversity of members" and ministries.[10] The liturgy is a dialogue between God and the Church. This dialogue is effected by the Spirit's activity informing and inspiring the coordinated ministry of all who form the liturgical assembly (children as well as adults, including its bishops, presbyters, deacons, readers, musicians, and acolytes).[11]

II. The Celebration of the Word of God with Children

Scripture Never Omitted

6. The Directory for Masses with Children clearly sets forth the Church's desire that children, no less than other members of the community, be formed by the same word of God. Therefore, at Masses with adults in which children also participate and at Masses with children in which only a few adults participate "biblical reading should never be omitted."[12]

Separate Liturgy of the Word

7. In Masses with adults in which children also participate, "[s]ometimes, moreover, if the place itself and the nature of the community permit, it will be appropriate to celebrate the liturgy of the word, including a homily, with the children in a separate, but not too distant, room."[13]

8. When children are to participate in the liturgy of the word in a space separate from the main assembly, they first gather with the rest of the assembly to celebrate the introductory rites. At the conclusion of the opening prayer, but before the first reading is proclaimed, the presiding priest may formally send the children and their ministers to the place where they will celebrate their own liturgy of the word. This may be done by presenting the Lectionary to the one who will preside over the liturgy of the word with the children and/or by words of dismissal, such as the following:

A Receive this book of readings
and proclaim God's word faithfully
to the children entrusted to your care.

B My dear children,
you will now go to hear God's word,
to praise God in song,
and to reflect on the wonderful things God has done for us.
We will await your return
so that together we may celebrate the eucharist.

At the conclusion of their liturgy of the word, and before the liturgy of the eucharist begins, the children return to their families.

Weekday Masses with Children

9. Although children are always to be led toward the parish's Sunday celebration of the eucharist, nevertheless, during the week Masses with children in which only a few adults participate are recommended.[14]

Homily or Explanation of the Readings

10. Because the explanation of the Scripture readings is so important at Masses with children, a homily should always be given. However, in order that they may not be deprived of the riches of God's word, especially if the priest finds it difficult to adapt himself to the mentality of children, and with the consent of the pastor or rector of the church, one of the adults participating in these celebrations may speak to the children after the gospel.[15]

III. The Lectionary for Masses with Children

A. ONE LECTIONARY

Purpose of Adaptation
11. This *Lectionary for Masses with Children* adheres as closely as possible to the selection and arrangement of readings for Sundays, solemnities, and feasts of the Lord in the *Lectionary for Mass*, while adapting them to the needs and capacities of children. In adapting the liturgy for use with children, the Church's goal is to nourish their faith and lead them to "active, conscious, and authentic" participation in the worship of the whole assembly,[16] but not to establish a different rite for children.[17]

Use of This Lectionary
12. In providing a lectionary for celebrations of the eucharist in which a considerable number of children are present, the Church intends to lead them into one community of faith, formed by the proclamation of the word of God. The scriptural readings contained in this Lectionary may be used at Sunday Masses when a large number of children are present along with adults, or when the children have a separate liturgy of the word, or for Masses at which most of the congregation consists of children (e.g., school Masses). The readings of this Lectionary are also a useful resource for those who wish to prepare other liturgical celebrations with children, and wish to do so within the context of the liturgical year.

13. Proper balance and consideration for the entire assembly should be observed. Therefore, priest celebrants should not use this *Lectionary for Masses with Children* exclusively or even preferentially at Sunday Masses, even though large numbers of children are present. In addition, this Lectionary may be used only when the liturgy of the word with the children is held in a place apart from the main assembly on Christmas Day, Epiphany, the Sundays of Lent, Easter Day, Ascension, and Pentecost. This is to ensure that on these days the Roman *Lectionary for Mass* will take precedence over the *Lectionary for Masses with Children* in the main assembly of the faithful.[18]

Family Preparation
14. Although the Church permits the liturgy of the word to be celebrated in a place apart from the main Sunday assembly,[19] it seeks to protect and foster the domestic church which is the Christian family.[20] This might be weakened if all the Scripture readings heard by parents were substantially different from those heard by their children on the same Sunday. This Lectionary is intended to encourage families to prepare together those readings which will be used in common both by the adults and the children for the celebration of the Sunday Mass (at least the gospel) and to reflect after the celebration on the word proclaimed there.

B. ADAPTED FOR PARTICULAR HEARERS OF THE WORD

Age Level
15. The hearers of the word for whom this work is primarily intended are children of elementary grades [preadolescents].[21]

Number of Readings
16. "If three or even two readings appointed on Sundays or weekdays can be understood by children only with difficulty, it is permissible to read two or only one of them, but the reading of the gospel should never be omitted."[22]

Omission of Readings
17. In the preparation of this Lectionary, readings from the *Lectionary for Mass* which were judged to be too abstract were eliminated or shortened.[23] Also omitted were passages of Scripture containing images that could confuse or disturb children, or readings children could perceive as anti-Semitic or racist.[24]

Length of Readings
18. Length was not the sole criterion for elimination or abridgment.[25] In particular cases longer or shorter forms of readings have been provided. Liturgical planners, with the consent of the priest celebrant, may further adapt particularly long readings by choosing to use only that part of the selection which presents a particular biblical image or is directly related to the other reading(s).

Replacement of Readings
19. When one of the first two readings for Sundays or solemnities or feasts of the Lord was judged inappropriate for children, it was omitted and not replaced with another. In cases where both of the two first readings in the Lectionary have been dropped, a replacement has been provided. The gospel selections appointed in the Roman *Lectionary for Mass* have been retained although in particular cases they have been shortened or otherwise adapted.

Responsorial Psalms
20. The responsorial psalms of the Lectionary have been adapted in order to foster the singing of these texts.[26] Some refrains and psalms have been shortened or replaced. For the most part, the responsorial psalms are related to the first reading.[27] To make it easier for the assembly to join in singing the responsorial psalm, some common texts have been provided for the liturgical seasons and for the commons of saints. These may be used in place of the assigned responsorial psalms when they are sung.[28]

C. THAT THE WORD OF GOD MIGHT BE PROCLAIMED IN THE LITURGICAL CELEBRATION

Worthy Celebration
21. The liturgy has the power to form children and all believers in the paschal mystery. The worthy celebration of the liturgy itself is the best introduction to liturgy.[29]

Bodily Involvement
22. In order to engage children's authentic participation, liturgy must respect their need for physical involvement. They should be invited to participate in the actions of the liturgy whenever it is appropriate and possible.[30] Their internal life is still very much dependent upon what they experience through their senses. Therefore, ritual elements such as gestures and postures, processions, song, dialogue, silence, and the use of symbols are integral to their experience of the liturgy.

Ministers
23. Children imitate the behaviors and attitudes of adults. For this reason, adults who serve as ministers at liturgical celebrations where children are present should conduct the entire range of liturgical actions, gestures, and

songs with dignity and care, yet without becoming distant or mechanical. All liturgical ministries are exercised for the sake of the prayer of the assembly. Therefore, ministers should be selected on the basis of liturgical competence. It should not be presumed that children should proclaim the word of God in the celebrations in which this Lectionary is used. Some younger children are able to read the Scriptures competently, but the witness of older children, teenagers, or adults, ministering graciously and reverently to young children engaged in liturgical prayer, is more conducive to the children's growing reverence for the word of God, than the peer ministry of embarrassed or ill-prepared children.[31]

Ritual Prayer
24. The Church's liturgy is first and foremost ritual prayer. The liturgy of the word is neither a catechetical session nor an introduction to biblical history. The liturgy celebrates the word of God in narrative and song, makes it visible in gesture and symbol, and culminates in the celebration of the eucharist.

D. THROUGHOUT THE LITURGICAL YEAR

Introduction: Calendars Express and Shape Identity
25. A calendar marks the celebrations which shape, carry on and expand a particular community's common life. This Lectionary, like the Roman *Lectionary for Mass* of which it is an adaptation, is based on the Church's calendar called the liturgical year. Its faithful observance is vital to Catholic identity. This is true for children no less than for adults. Faithful observance of the calendar promotes formation and participation in the life of the Church.

Paschal Mystery
26. The Sundays, seasons and feasts of the liturgical year celebrate many facets of a single mystery. Each of them expresses from a different perspective the one great mystery of Christ's dying and rising yesterday, today and for ever. The mystery of redemption effected by Christ's incarnation, death, and resurrection is grounded in historical events of the past, yet leads to a future glory not yet fully revealed. The entire mystery, however, is present: God is now creating and redeeming in Christ. Each day Christ's Church is dying and coming to new life in him through the indwelling of the Spirit given at baptism. In ritual prayer, past and future are caught up into God's eternal present. Hence the liturgy is not an historical pageant trying to recreate a long-past event but rather is a true participation in Christ's death and resurrection, the paschal mystery. An understanding and appropriation of this mystery provides the essential starting point for preparing and celebrating the Church's liturgy.

Sunday
27. The shaping of time in the Church's tradition is related to the rhythms of nature, e.g., the relationship of morning and evening prayer to the daily rising and setting of the sun. The most fundamental shape of liturgical time, however, is the week. The first day of the week, Sunday, is the Lord's Day on which Christians assemble to celebrate the paschal mystery whose fullest expression is the celebration of the eucharist. Although it may be possible in appropriate ways to integrate a civil, diocesan, parochial, or domestic celebration within the Sunday liturgy, the full assembly's celebration of the Sunday eucharist must always take precedence over other special occasions. Fidelity to the Lectionary on Sundays, whether during the seasons or in Ordinary Time, is an indispensable element of Catholic formation. This Lectionary contains the readings for all the Sundays of the liturgical year in each year of the three-year cycle of readings.

Weekdays

28. In addition to the readings for Sunday, this Lectionary provides thirty-six sets of readings for the weekdays in Ordinary Time. All four gospels are represented in these weekday selections. The readings provided for the weekdays of each season are generally taken from the respective Sundays and weekdays of the *Lectionary for Mass* so that the images fundamental to the understanding and celebration of that season are adequately represented. Each set of readings has a heading which points out the dominant theme of the readings.

The Seasons: Easter Triduum, Season of Easter, and Season of Lent

29. THE TRIDUUM — The Easter Triduum or three days "begins with the evening Mass of the Lord's Supper on Holy Thursday, reaches its high point in the Easter Vigil, and closes with evening prayer on Easter Sunday."[32] The Sunday by Sunday celebration of our life in Christ finds its culmination in this annual celebration of Christ's passover from death to new life. These three days are best understood and celebrated as one liturgy which in its totality celebrates the paschal mystery. The liturgies of each day highlight the different facets of this mystery.

30. The duplication of the liturgies of Holy Thursday and Good Friday is permitted only with the permission of the Ordinary and, in the case of the Easter Vigil, is prohibited. These liturgies have a power and simplicity all of their own. No provision is made for a separate liturgy of the word for children on these occasions and this Lectionary has not provided adapted readings for these occasions. Nevertheless, care should be taken to insure that participation by children in these celebrations is both encouraged and fostered.

31. The united proclamation of Christ's death and resurrection first sounds in the entrance song of the Evening Mass of the Lord's Supper: "We should glory in the cross of our Lord Jesus Christ, for he is our salvation, our life and our resurrection; through him we are saved and made free."[33] It intensifies in the antiphon at the veneration of the cross on Good Friday: "We worship you, Lord, we venerate your cross, we praise your resurrection. Through the cross you brought joy to the world." It climaxes in the Easter Vigil Preface: "We praise you with greater joy than ever on this Easter night when Christ became our paschal sacrifice." It echoes in the reading for Evening Prayer of Easter Sunday, the closing liturgy of the Triduum: "Christ has offered one single sacrifice for sins. . . . By virtue of that one single offering he has achieved the eternal perfection of all whom he is sanctifying."[34]

32. The Easter Triduum should reflect our deepest belief that Christ has died once for all and that Holy Thursday evening, Good Friday and Holy Saturday are as much celebrations of the Lord's paschal mystery as is Easter Sunday, although each of these days may focus upon a particular aspect of that mystery which cannot be separated from the others.

33. THE SEASON OF EASTER — Following ancient tradition, the Church celebrates Easter for fifty days, from Easter Sunday to Pentecost. These fifty days are understood to be and are celebrated as one "great Sunday."[35] The Scripture readings, liturgical texts, and rites of these fifty days take precedence over civil, school, diocesan, parochial, or domestic celebrations. These events may be integrated with the celebration of the season of Easter, but this should be done with great care.

34. The primacy of the celebration of the Sundays of Easter is rooted in the traditional character of this period as a time for ongoing catechesis, especially in regard to the sacraments of initiation (baptism, confirmation, and eucharist) and to the deeper spiritual meaning of the liturgical rites. This particular expression of the Church's formation process is called mystagogy.[36] Since most children have been baptized as infants and have received or soon will receive the eucharist, it is appropriate to draw out the meaning of these initiatory sacraments for the children during this season.

35. Throughout the season of Easter the first reading is from the Acts of the Apostles. In a three-year cycle of parallel and progressive selections, material is presented on the life of the primitive Church, its witness and growth.[37] For the second reading, passages are taken from I Peter in Year A, I John in Year B, the Revelation of John in Year C. "These are the texts that seem to fit in especially well with the spirit of joyous faith and sure hope proper to this season."[38] The gospel selections for the first three Sundays of Easter recount the appearances of the risen Christ. On the Fourth Sunday, the gospel is that of the Good Shepherd; on the Fifth, Sixth, and Seventh Sundays the Lord's discourse and prayer at the Last Supper are read. Eight sets of readings are provided for the weekdays of the Easter season.

36. THE SEASON OF LENT — Lent extends from Ash Wednesday until just before the Holy Thursday Mass of the Lord's Supper. This season is a period of preparation for the celebration of the Easter Triduum.

37. The season of Lent takes its shape and meaning from the process and rites of conversion which lead to baptism. The process of initiation gave birth to the forty days of Lent. The privileged nature of the Triduum and the joyous celebration of Easter for fifty days can be adequately understood and maintained in worship only if Lent has led the community to the realization that this season celebrates the very nature of Christian life. As catechumens are enrolled on the First Sunday of Lent for baptism at the Easter Vigil, the word of God calls all Christians — children as well as adults — back to a deeper appreciation of their own baptism.

38. The readings, prayers, and Lenten seasonal practices are ultimately to be interpreted and celebrated in the light of our baptism into Christ's dying and rising. The gospels for the first two Sundays of Lent in all three cycles recount the Lord's temptation and transfiguration. The readings of Year A for the Third, Fourth, and Fifth Sundays of Lent are of major importance to Christian initiation and are always used when the Scrutinies are celebrated and may also be used in Years B and C even when there are no catechumens in the parish. "The Old Testament readings are about the history of salvation, which is one of the themes proper to the catechesis of Lent. The series of texts for each year presents the main elements of salvation history from its beginning until the promise of the New Covenant."[39] For the season of Lent only three selections from the letters of the apostles are included in this Lectionary. As in the *Lectionary for Mass*, these selections correspond to the gospel. Nine sets of readings are provided for the weekdays of Lent.

The Seasons: Advent – Christmas

39. THE SEASON OF ADVENT — The first part of the Advent season extends from the First Sunday of Advent through December 16. The second part extends from December 17 through December 24.

40. The reign of God is already among us but is not yet made manifest in its fullness. As Christians, we celebrate what already is while standing in expectation of what is yet to be revealed. Though we cannot bring about the fullness of God's reign through our efforts alone we can cooperate with God's grace to be ready and vigilant for its advent (coming). The Advent season is one of vigilant waiting but not of Lenten penitence. The first part of the season of Advent directs the eyes of our faith to the fullness yet to be revealed when the Spirit-inspired vision of the prophets, especially Isaiah and John the Baptist, will become full reality. The second part prepares us to celebrate Christ's coming in the flesh at Bethlehem. This sense of vigilance and expectation should not be anticipated by civil, diocesan, parochial, or school celebrations of Christmas during the season of Advent.

41. The Sunday gospels in Advent treat the Lord's coming at the end of time (First Sunday of Advent), John the Baptist (Second and Third Sundays), and the events that immediately prepare for the Lord's birth (Fourth Sunday). The Old Testament readings, especially those from Isaiah, are prophecies about the Messiah and the Messianic age. The readings from the apostles serve as exhortations and as proclamations, in keeping with the different themes of Advent.[40] For the weekdays of Advent this Lectionary provides four sets of readings which reflect some of the major themes of the season.

42. The Season of Christmas — This season begins on the Vigil of Christmas and ends with the Feast of the Baptism of the Lord. The inauguration of the fullness we await was at long last disclosed in the incarnation and birth of Jesus (Christmas), born of Mary (Solemnity of Mary, Mother of God), who became a part of a human family (Feast of the Holy Family), was manifested to the nations (Epiphany), and revealed as God's own beloved child (Baptism of the Lord). The Christmas season celebrates the appearance of God among us in the birth, epiphany, and baptism of the Lord Jesus: the beginning of our salvation in Christ.

43. Christmas does not merely celebrate the birth of a child, rather this great feast celebrates the incarnation (birth) of the Lord of history in our world as God's own Word in our very flesh. It is the beginning of the paschal mystery and inevitably leads to his saving passion and resurrection from the dead. The full cycle of Christmas feasts, as surely as the celebration of the Easter Triduum, proclaims that God's "eternal Word has taken upon himself our human weakness."[41]

44. This is evident in the Gospel infancy narratives which, rather than being merely stories about the birth of a child, are anticipations of the acceptance and rejection which Jesus would meet throughout his ministry and unto his very death. Therefore Christmas is as integral to an adult understanding of faith as is Easter. Just as the Easter Triduum is one three-day celebration of Christ's paschal mystery, so the various feasts of the Christmas season are themselves celebrations of that same mystery made manifest in human history from the first moment of Jesus' birth. It is especially appropriate that the celebration of Christmas be prolonged throughout the Christmas season, rather than anticipating it as is so common in secular culture.

45. Only one set of readings for Christmas is provided in this Lectionary. These readings may be used for the Mass of the vigil, at midnight, at dawn, or during the day.

Ordinary Time
46. Ordinary Time comprises the thirty-three or thirty-four weeks of the liturgical year which follow the major seasons of Christmas and Easter. There are two periods of Ordinary Time: one which extends from the end of the Christmas season to the beginning of Lent; a longer one which extends from the end of the Easter season to the beginning of Advent. Ordinary Time is devoted to the mystery of Christ in all its aspects.[42] During these weeks the Gospel accounts of Jesus' ministry and teaching are proclaimed and celebrated. This Lectionary provides thirty-nine sets of readings for use on the weekdays in Ordinary Time. All four gospels are represented in these weekday selections.

The Proper of Saints
47. Throughout the centuries the Church has kept holy the memory of Mary, Mother of God, the apostles, the martyrs, and all the saints. The liturgy presents these men and women to us as intercessors and models. The entire Church joins in the celebrations of saints of universal significance, whereas other saints may be commemorated with optional celebrations by local churches or religious families.

48. Children's openness to the power of stories makes them ready listeners when they hear stories of the saints, the examples of whose lives give them a deeper appreciation of the gospel. This is especially true in the stories of saints of our time and nation. This Lectionary provides readings for all solemnities and for many feasts. Common readings are provided for use on other feasts and memorials.

IV. Particular Issues

Place of Celebration
49. The place where the liturgy of the word is celebrated may influence how the children receive God's word. It should be chosen carefully. Sometimes a space outside the usual place of worship may need to be chosen.[43] Even when classrooms or other non-liturgical spaces must be used for celebrations of the word with children every care must be taken that these spaces be well prepared, and that the environment is suitable for the worship of God.

The Lectionary and Other Objects Used in the Celebration
50. By their beauty and by the reverent way in which they are carried and handled the books used for the celebration of the word of God should be eloquent witnesses to the Church's reverence for the Scriptures.[44] The proclamation of the word transcends the mere communication of information and becomes a community-building celebration of God's saving mystery especially when candles, incense, banners, and processions magnify the word's impact on eyes and ears, in hearts and minds.

Music
51. The eucharistic liturgy requires the full use of music which is integral to the whole celebration, including the proclamation of the word of God. The responsorial psalm is normally sung by a cantor with the assembly singing the refrain. The gospel acclamation must always be sung. A sung response to the petitions of the general intercessions can enhance participation.

Plays within the Liturgy of the Word

52. The Mass is not an historical reenactment of the events of salvation history and care should be taken not to give the impression that the liturgy of the word is a play. This is not to say that dramatic elements may not be used, e.g., the readings may at times be divided into parts distributed among the children;[45] however, the use of costumes, etc., is more appropriate in the context of other celebrations or services. Care should be taken especially at Christmas and during Holy Week and the Easter Triduum not to stage the various liturgies as plays. The Christmas Mass should not be presented as a birthday party for Jesus, nor should secular notions of Santa Claus be introduced into the Christmas liturgy.

Common Format

53. The preparation and celebration of liturgies for children begin with and flow from a clear desire to assist them to participate in the worship of the entire community. This is best accomplished when the basic shape of the ritual used with the children, its symbols, gestures, and language, is similar to that of the full assembly. The children are thus enabled to celebrate the paschal mystery of Christ on their own level of understanding and are led to the celebration of those same mysteries in the full assembly of the faithful.

CONCLUSION

54. Christ's particular care for children teaches us that they are capable of welcoming God's call and responding to it. Children's human and, therefore, religious experience is complete and whole in itself and is not determined simply by their potential for adulthood. The fullest reality of the liturgical assembly is children and adults together — not separate celebrations which run the risk of diminishing the place of children in the liturgical assembly. It should be noted that the same thing can happen if inadequate attention is given to their presence in the full assembly. Nevertheless, there will be occasions when a particular assembly is constituted almost entirely of children and other occasions where their numbers are so significant that the adaptations suggested by the Directory for Masses with Children should be applied for the sake of good pastoral care. This adaptation of the *Lectionary for Mass* is intended further to help those ministering to children. For them it provides the opportunity for deeper conversion as they attend to these young hearers of the word. The way in which the word of God is proclaimed and celebrated in the lives of children today will shape the future life of the Church.

NOTES

1. See John 1:1 – 3,14.
2. See Hebrews 1:1 – 3.
3. Lectionary for Mass [OLM], Introduction, no. 4.
4. See Matthew 18:19 – 20; see also Constitution on the Liturgy, *Sacrosanctum Concilium* [SC], art. 7.
5. See SC, art. 7.
6. See Directory for Masses with Children [DMC], no. 8.
7. See OLM, no. 6 and DMC, no. 15.
8. See SC, art. 24, 35, and 56.
9. See SC, art. 2; see also OLM, no. 10.
10. OLM, no. 8.
11. See DMC, nos. 22 – 24.
12. DMC, no. 41.
13. Ibid., no. 17.
14. See DMC, nos. 20 – 21.
15. DMC, no. 24.
16. Ibid., no. 12.
17. See DMC, nos. 3 and 21.
18. See letter of the Congregation for Divine Worship and the Discipline of the Sacraments granting permission for the experimental use of the *Lectionary for Masses with Children* (Prot. N. 1259/91).
19. See DMC, no. 17.
20. See DMC, no. 16.
21. See DMC, no. 6.
22. DMC, no. 42.
23. See DMC, nos. 42 – 43.
24. See DMC, no. 43.
25. See DMC, no. 44.
26. See DMC, no. 30.
27. See DMC, no. 46.
28. See OLM, Introduction, no. 9.
29. See DMC, no. 12.
30. See DMC, nos. 33 and 34.
31. See DMC, no. 24.
32. See General Norms for the Liturgical Year and the Calendar [GNLYC], no. 19.
33. Galatians 6:14.
34. Hebrews 10:12 – 14.
35. See GNLYC, no. 22.
36. Rite of Christian Initiation of Adults, no. 247.
37. See OLM, no. 100.
38. OLM, no. 100.
39. OLM, no. 97.
40. See OLM, no. 93.
41. *Roman Missal* (*Sacramentary*), Preface of Christmas III.
42. GNLYC, no. 43.
43. See DMC, no. 25.
44. See OLM, no. 35.
45. See DMC, no. 47.

INDEX OF
SCRIPTURE READINGS
IN THE LECTIONARY FOR MASSES WITH CHILDREN

Use this index as a way to locate appropriate texts from the *Lectionary for Masses with Children.*

The numbers following the letters are lectionary numbers, not page numbers. Many of the summary lines have been simplified for use in this index. Readings that vary only slightly have often been placed on a single line.

A, B, C and W refer to the volumes of the *Lectionary for Masses with Children:* Year A, Year B, Year C and Weekdays.

Isaiah (continued)

Jeremiah

Matthew (continued)

Matthew (continued)

Mark

Luke

Luke (continued)

John

1 Corinthians
1:3 – 9 **B**2 The revelation we looked for, Christ Jesus.
1:10 – 13, 17 **A**62 Be of one mind.
1:26 – 31 **A**65, **W**470 God has chosen what seems weak.
2:1 – 5 **A**68 I have announced to you Christ crucified.
2:6 – 10 **A**71 What no eye has seen.
3:18 – 20 **A**74 The world's wisdom is foolishness.
5:6b – 8 **A**36, **B**36, **C**36 Look to the things above.
9:16 – 18 **B**69 I must preach the gospel.
10:16 – 17 **A**161 Though we are many, we are one bread.
10:31 — 11:1 **B**72 Be imitators of me, as I am of Christ.
11:23 – 26 **C**163 The eucharistic meal.
12:4 – 7, 12 – 13 or 12:12 – 13 **A**58, **B**58, **C**58, **W**475 Baptized in one body.
12:4 – 11 or 12:4 – 13 **C**61, **W**480 Many gifts, one spirit.
12:12 – 13 or 12:12 – 14, 27 **W**225, **C**64 Together you are Christ's body.
13:4 – 7 **W**194 Love is the greatest gift.
13:4 – 8a, 11 – 13 **C**67 Faith, hope and love.
13:4 – 13 **W**470 Love never ends.
15:3 – 8, 11 **C**70 We preached Christ and you believed.
15:12, 16 – 20 **C**73 If Christ is not risen, your faith is in vain.
15:20 – 24a **A**155 Christ will hand over the kingdom to the Father.

2 Corinthians
1:3 – 4 **W**175 Our merciful God always comforts us.
4:6 – 11 **B**81 The life of Jesus is revealed in our body.
4:16 — 5:1 **B**84 We have a house not made with hands.
5:6 – 10 **B**87 Walk by faith, not by sight.
5:14 – 17 **B**90 All things are made new.
5:17 – 19 **C**29 God reconciled us through Christ.
6:4 – 10 **W**457 We are said to be dying and yet we are alive.
8:1 – 3a, 12 **W**209 They were glad to give generously.
8:7, 9, 13 – 14 **B**93 Your abundance should supply their want.
9:8 – 11 **W**519 God will provide bread for people to eat.
12:7 – 10 **B**96 In my weakness is the power of Christ.
13:11 – 13 **A**158 The grace of Lord Jesus Christ be with you.

Galatians
1:11 – 12, 15 – 19 **C**85 Paul's mission.
3:26 – 28 or 3:26 – 29 **W**475, **C**91 You have put on Christ.
5:1, 13 – 15 **C**94 You were called to freedom.
5:22 – 23, 25 – 26 **W**223 The Spirit has given us life.

Ephesians
1:3 – 5 or 1:3 – 6 or 1:3 – 10 **W**532, **W**448, **B**99 God chose us.
1:15 – 16a, 18 – 19a **W**205 Know the hope to which God calls you.
1:17 – 21 **A**52, **B**53, **C**54 God seated Jesus at the right hand in heaven.
2:4 – 10 **B**28 Christ brought us to life.
2:20 – 22 **W**443, **W**452 The whole building is bound together.
3:14 – 19 **B**165 The love of Christ is beyond all knowledge.
3:16b – 17, 20 – 21 **W**231 Christ's power is at work in our hearts.
4:1 – 6 or 4:1 – 7 **B**105, **W**466 One body, one Lord, one faith, one baptism.
4:11 – 13 **W**466 The different gifts are to build unity.
4:31 — 5:2 **B**111 Walk in love, just as in Christ.
5:1 – 2, 8 – 10 **A**27, **W**488 You are people of light.
5:8 – 10 **W**193 Make your light shine.
5:15 – 20 **B**114 Be watchful that you may know God's will.
6:1 – 4 **B**117 Honor your father and your mother.
6:18b – 19a, 20b **W**220 Pray always by the power of the Spirit.

LTP's Resource Bibliography

FOR PREPARING LITURGY WITH CHILDREN

All of these titles are available from Liturgy Training Publications:

Children in the Assembly of the Church. Eleanor Bernstein, CSJ, and John Brooks-Leonard, eds. 1993. Fundamental questions are explored in these essays.

Children's Daily Prayer. Elizabeth McMahon Jeep. Annual. In its own words, "a liturgy of the hours for the classroom with an order of prayer for each school day."

Companion to the Calendar. Mary Ellen Hynes. 1993. Lively information about all the seasons and special days of the church's year.

Hymnal for Catholic Students. Copublished with GIA. Songs every Christian should learn. Useful tapes, accompaniments and arrangements are also available.

Leader's Manual of the *Hymnal for Catholic Students.* Gabe Huck and others. 1989. An introduction to liturgy written especially for teachers. Includes recommendations for feast days during the school year.

Lectionary for Masses with Children, ritual editions and study editions, with volumes for Years A, B and C, and for weekdays. 1993. Compiled by the United States Catholic Conference for the Committee on the Liturgy of the National Conference of Catholic Bishops.

Liturgy and Appointment Calendar: A Desk Calendar for Parish and School. Annual.

The Liturgy Documents: A Parish Resource, third edition. Elizabeth Hoffman, ed. 1991. The most useful documents of the liturgical reform.

Liturgy with Style and Grace. Gabe Huck. 1984. Practical guidelines for every liturgical minister.

The Religious Potential of the Child. Sophia Cavelletti. 1992. A classic.

Sourcebook for Sundays and Seasons: An Almanac of Parish Liturgy. An annual handbook for the preparation of worship.

Take Me Home: Notes on the Church Year for Children. Christine Kenny-Sheputis. 1991. Weekly notes about feasts and seasons to photocopy and to send home with students.

The Welcome Table: Planning Masses with Children. Elizabeth McMahon Jeep, ed. 1982. Sensible and sound.

The Year of Grace: A Liturgical Calendar, poster size (26" square) or notebook size. Annual.

Worksheet for Preparing Mass

MINISTERS

presider:

cantor or leader of song:

other musicians:

reader(s):

homilist:

cantor or reader of intercessions:

eucharistic ministers:

WHO WILL CARRY THESE ITEMS?

cross:

lectionary:

incense:

candles:

banners:

wine:

bread:

gifts for those in need:

* * * * *

INTRODUCTORY RITES

Opening Song *(a communal song or psalm related to the season or feast celebrated that day):*

Penitential Rite *(or sprinkling rite, especially on Sundays and during Eastertime):*

Glory to God *(only on Sundays [except in Advent and Lent], on solemnities and on feasts):*

LITURGY OF THE WORD

First Reading:

Psalm:

Second Reading *(on Sundays and solemnities there may be a second reading):*

Gospel Acclamation *(an alleluia sung by everyone, with a verse sung by a cantor; during Lent another acclamation replaces the alleluia)*

alleluia or acclamation:

verse:

Gospel:

Profession of Faith *(only on Sundays and solemnities):*

General Intercessions *(introduced by the presider, sung or read by a cantor or reader, and concluded with a prayer by the presider)*

response to the intercessions:

intercessions:

LITURGY OF THE EUCHARIST

Preparation of the Altar and the Gifts *(instrumental music, a solo song, a communal song, or silence)*

musicians/singers:

choice of music:

Acclamations of the Eucharistic Prayer *(Holy, holy, holy; memorial acclamation; and Great Amen; or other acclamations):*

Litany at the Breaking of the Bread *(Lamb of God):*

Communion Song *(a communal song or psalm appropriate to communion):*

CONCLUDING RITE

Recessional *(instrumental music, a communal song, or silence):*

 This worksheet can be duplicated for your use. It can be enlarged 125% to fit on 8½ × 11″ paper.